Rejuvenate Your
Golf Skills

Golf Skills to Last

John Snow

Outskirts Press, Inc.
Denver, Colorado

Rejuvenate Your Golf Skills
Golf Skills to Last
All Rights Reserved.
Copyright © 2009 John Snow
V2.0

Outskirts Press, Inc.
http://www.outskirtspress.com

ISBN: 978-1-4327-2150-3

Outskirts Press and the "OP" logo are trademarks belonging to Outskirts Press, Inc.

PRINTED IN THE UNITED STATES OF AMERICA

This book is dedicated to my wife, Nancy, for her love and support that she brings into my life.

PREFACE

What will this book do for you?

Rejuvenate Your Golf Skills describes simple and clear methods to develop a set of golf skills to last a lifetime. If you are an avid golfer experiencing the slow recovery process from shoulder or back surgery, this book is for you. If you are recovering from knee or hip surgery, this book is for you. If you are a retiree returning to the game or a beginning golfer, this book is for you.

The steps and methods described in this book are intended to assist a person recovering from surgery to get back to the game. The post-surgery period can be long and very boring. The steps described in this book allow one to start with simple motions to get back to the game's fundamentals and advance as one's recovery permits.

Technique descriptions start with putting and then

advance to chip and pitch shots. It is important to obtain a shot feeling and an eye for accuracy at the beginning of one's experience. This is followed by low stress/impact wedge and short-iron shots, which must reach the green to score and enjoy this great game. Subsequently, hybrids, fairway metals, and driver shots are addressed. I would suggest that one not progress to longer clubs until one understands and feels shot execution methods and achieves confidence with the shorter clubs.

My objective is to describe the steps I took during my post-surgery period that resulted in significant improvements in shot execution and lower scores.

Part One

Golf Skills

FOREWORD

The attraction to the game of golf is the opportunity each shot presents as a challenge to our mental and physical capabilities. Golf enables our best and worst characteristics to rise through the game's accomplishments and failures. Before one can enjoy the unique challenges of courses and specific golf holes, basic shot skills should be developed for one's complete enjoyment of the game.

I am not a golf professional or a golf swing coach, nor do I believe I am an expert in golf skills. I am a retired engineer with 39 years of systems engineering and product development experience. I have read more than 70 golf instruction books and have studied the nuances of the golf game for 30 years. I searched through many golf instruction and sports fitness books and Web sites looking for simple and clear advice to rebuild a swing after surgery. I wanted to increase my understanding of the subtle characteristics and methodology necessary to execute quality golf shots that are repeatable. Most golf books are single-topic books on the full swing. There are a few books on bunker shots. Some of the golf book authors articulate their ideas very effectively and others ineffectively.

I wanted one quality reference for learning and maintaining a solid golf skill foundation. I could not find an all-inclusive reference that describes how to build a golf swing or, more importantly, a golf skill foundation from the green back to the tee box. I made copious notes of the key points during a comprehensive investigation; the results were organized and structured into sections three through five of this golf skills guidance. Sections one, two, six, and seven were added later to make a complete document.

While creating this document I learned more with regard to shot-making; while practicing the steps for each shot and swing type I gained more experience. I can feel the club head as I make the short shots. I have a better appreciation and confidence for how to get the ball close to the hole from less than 100 yards.

MY GOLF BACKGROUND

I have played golf for 36 years; I have played with shoulder problems for nearly ten years. I would take two Advil or two Aleve before each golf round. I would take Advil or Aleve when doing any type of moderate yard work or house maintenance. I thought this was normal for people over 50 years old.

When I was 50 years old, my golf handicap was +5.4; I had a very nice year. I worked rather hard on swing tempo and short-game basics for two years to reach that milestone. Subsequently work interfered with golf and golf practice. I restarted playing golf weekly in 2006; the shoulder aches reappeared as I attempted to play on a regular basis. My best round in 2007 was a 73 [+1] on a hot summer day in July. Looking back, the hot day allowed my shoulder to loosen up for a good swing. My shoulder aches increased in intensity and occurrence during the 2007 golfing season. This pain restricted my shoulder turn and my ability to raise the club, so my scores started to climb. I stopped playing golf on a regular basis in November 2007. At the beginning of 2008, an MRI indicated severe rotator cuff tears as well as a disconnected bicep tendon.

My surgery was on 26 March 2008 by an excellent surgeon, Dr. James Dreese, at the Kernan Hospital in Baltimore, Maryland. My physical therapy started on 2 April 2008 at Bayside PT & Sports Rehabilitation with excellent therapists. The physical therapy continued for 24 weeks after surgery. What did I want to achieve by rebuilding my golf swing after shoulder surgery?

- Repeatable balanced golf swing with smooth tempo
- Excellent short game, know and feel specific chip and pitch shots
- Make 60% of putts < 4 foot in length

Why did I want to improve my golf skills?

I wanted the personal satisfaction of reaching a defined goal and achieving a higher skill level as well as increasing the enjoyment and satisfaction of each round.

Introduction

Objective

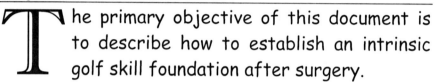

The primary objective of this document is to describe how to establish an intrinsic golf skill foundation after surgery.

Purpose

This document follows the physical limitations of a golfer following shoulder surgery and uses that to an advantage for purposes of relearning golf skills. Recovery from shoulder surgery is a long and slow process. Rather than focus on the limited motion and strength capabilities following surgery, I focused on the positive aspects of this limitation. This recovery period provides a fantastic opportunity to occupy the time with short-game fundamentals.

Research

It seems that most shots executed by amateur, average, and professional golfers are within 100 yards of the green. During an 18-hole round, approximately 70% of an average golfer's shots (66 of 94) are in the scoring zone, < 100 yards to the green. The 70% includes putts, bunker shots, chip, and pitch shots. It seems like acquiring a feel and skill for short-iron shots should be a priority to improving one's handicap.

The table No.1.1 below illustrates the average shot types per game per handicap type golfer.

Table No.1.1:Typical Golfer Shot Types per Round

GOLFER	SCORE	PUTTS	FULL SHOTS	SHORT GAME
Tour	71	28	26	17
Scratch	72	30	27	15
10 Handicap	83	34	25	24
20 Handicap	94	36	28	30
30 Handicap	105	39	29	37

In my view, amateur golfers are scratch golfers who compete in competitive golf. Most average golfers have handicaps that are greater than ten. The average golfer does not spend very much time practicing the short game. Most average golfers must attend to their family and career ahead of the recreational activities.

Priorities have not changed for the average golfer over the last several decades, if anything, pressures of the current fast-paced society put more demands on golfers' time at work and at home. When they do have a small amount of time for practice they head to the driving range to hit middle irons, fairway woods, and the big dog. Close to zero time is spent on putting or chip and pitch shots. I should point out that there are very few driving ranges or golf courses with short-game practice areas or practice bunkers set aside for public access.

It seems ironic that when one has raised a family, the professional career is nearing the twilight phase, and as time for golf and golf practice increases, the youthful flexibility and strength have escaped one's body. Most of us who increase physical activities after many years of observing it rather than participating are susceptible to physical injury. Building or rebuilding a solid golf foundation after injury and/or surgery should be viewed as an opportunity to enhance one's enjoyment of the game for a lifetime.

Spending 50% of one's practice time on acquiring a

short-game skill and maintaining it would pay significant dividends. One to two hours per month could easily change a double bogey golfer into a bogey golfer.

Organization

This book has two parts: Part One describes how to rebuild a golf swing after surgery. Part Two discusses factors that influence an average golfer's ability to score on the course.

Part One of this book's organization describes in a sequential manner the steps necessary to develop a solid golf skill foundation. This set of building blocks starts with putts, progresses to chips and pitches, then short irons, hybrids, fairway metals, and finally to a driver.

Within each guidance subsection, key points related to setup, alignment, and swing dynamics are addressed. I wanted to achieve skills with short-and moderate-length putts, chips, and pitches while the shoulder was healing and there was little possibility of over stressing the tendons. Recording the average chip and pitch shot distances, after gaining confidence with shot repeatability, provides skill visibility and a reference for the future rounds. The same is true for short iron, hybrid, and fairway metal shot skills and fly distances.

Section Three is devoted to developing shot skills on the green, around the green, on the fairway, and within bunkers to lower one's score. When working on short irons, hybrids, and fairway metal shots, use the full-swing guidance within Section Four to execute half and full swings.

Section Four concentrates on the details to developing a solid full swing. Focus is on coiling and uncoiling the upper torso, swing engine, with a balanced and smooth swing tempo.

Section Five looks at pre-shot routines, shot adjustments during a round, and round record keeping. Section Six describes key mental benefits to working hard to achieve one's goals and some physical considerations. Section Seven discusses methods to maintain your swing tempo and a pace of play while playing golf rounds.

Part Two of this book is subdivided into nine areas

to address factors that can improve and influence an average golfer's ability to score well and enjoy each round.

Golf Game Goals

I wanted to increase the quality of my short game so that the following primary objectives were obtainable. Bunker shot practice must wait until six months after the doctor's release to play golf.

Ultimate Goal: Single Digit Handicap
Primary Objectives:

Full Swing	Hit Target Areas > 80%
Approach Shot	Greens in Regulation > 60%
Short Game	Pitch and Chip to < 9 feet to Hole
Putting	< 32 Putts / Round
Mental	Isolate Thoughts to Only Current Shot

SECTION TWO

Swing Development Plan

T he plan's structure is organized with respect to increasing flexibility and strength training of the shoulder.

Approach

The "Detailed Golf Skill Guidance" section is the primary section for building a quality golf skill foundation. It starts with the putter and progresses through the golf tool set to the driver. This section suggests methods and many practice sessions to acquire shot-making skills.

The "Full Golf Swing Guidance" section explains how to execute a typical full swing. Attention is placed on setup, swing tempo, and a balanced swing.

It is important to read section four after the chip shot subsection and prior to practicing the wedge, short iron, hybrid, and fairway metal shots. Understanding the swing techniques for a quality swing tempo, core rotation, wrist actions, and a balanced swing are extremely important for all shots.

The "Game Guidance" section suggests methods [my methods] for creating a game strategy, a pre-shot routine, and record keeping.

The format for the skill and swing guidance sections is close to a task description style rather than free-flowing text. My goal was to provide significant information in a concise manner for each shot type.

The shot techniques in this document describe the fundamentals of a balanced golf swing. The essential shot objectives, key points, setup, swing, club options, shot record, and practice sessions are delineated for each shot type.

I have also described how I see each shot executed. The practice drills are proven methods to learn a specific shot technique for game improvement; they worked for me.

Practice will be the primary activity while the shoulder tendons and muscles are recovering from surgery. The physical therapist and the body seriously restrict the use of the shoulder, and then there is the body's feedback network—pain. This is a marvelous opportunity to build a golf skill foundation, starting with putting, advancing through near green, and close to green shots to fairway shots and finally to tee shots. I had many weeks to work on the near green shots and develop a skill set.

Training Aids — All available training aids should be used to assist in this detailed approach to rebuilding a golf swing. A putting mat and a practice swing mat can be used at home for regular practice. A weighted grip-training club can be used to practice static swing positions. The Medicus hinged five iron and a Medicus hinged driver are very good tools for building a swing tempo and swing path. A Speed Stik and a Momentus weighted swing club are good tools for very slowly building flexibility and strength in the arm, shoulder, and back muscles.

Development Schedule

The initial development schedule, Illustration No.1, was created by gathering snippets of information from many sports therapy Internet sites that addressed recovery from shoulder operations. These snippets are integrated and organized into a sequential order that paralleled the shoulder recovery period.

I must say several things regarding recovery from major surgery, rehabilitation, and physical recovery.

- If the bicep was ruptured and reattached or if you had severe SLAP tears repaired, the recovery could be two to three months longer than illustrated.
- If you are recovering from shoulder, back, knee, or hip surgery, increase swing skill development efforts only as recommended by your sports therapist.
- We are all different and our recovery progress will be different from one another. Some differences are due to complexity of surgery, healing process, exercise diligence, and overall attitude.
- When starting to chip or advance to another shot type, begin with very slow short swings; stop at the first indication of pain. I stopped

several times and waited one to two weeks before increasing distance or speed.

- The body has a unique system to let you know if muscles, tendons, or joints are being stressed too soon—pain.
- The overall golf swing rehabilitation period illustrated is approximately in the middle between the optimistic and conservative approaches to post shoulder surgery rehabilitation.

Putting - I started to practice at home out of boredom at week six. I could only practice for about 15 minutes. I made sure the putter was supported mostly by the good shoulder/arm. Letting the recovering arm hang unsupported would cause it to ache substantially, so I would stop for approximately one hour to rest the shoulder. I practiced for two 15-minute sessions the first couple of days and later added a third session.

Chipping - Practice started at home, on a soft mat, at week nine with very slow motions. I wanted to feel the swing and ensure myself that I was not causing any stress to the shoulder. Practice was limited to 15-minute sessions for the same reasons as the putter sessions. Swinging very slowly allowed me to feel the club head and observe the clubface position at the impact point. I marked the mat with a line to indicate the ball position. Home practice also enabled me to work on setup and alignment to have the clubface square at impact.

At week ten, I went to the local public course to practice putting and chipping. The sessions were limited to avoid any severe aches. I would rest the arm every 15 minutes for approximately 15 minutes. The sessions were very pleasant because I was outside enjoying the fresh air and sun. Making very slow swings with the putter and eight iron enabled me to feel the club head and appreciate solid contact. I did not increase swing speed until week 13.

Pitching - The pitch swing started at home in week ten with very slow and limited back and forward swings. The emphasis was on feeling the club head and observing the clubface position at the impact point. I started practicing five- and ten-yard pitch shots with slow swings at week 11. I placed the ball on top of the grass for at least two weeks to protect the shoulder from any additional stress.

I continued practicing putting, chipping, and pitching short distances for several weeks while the physical therapy was increasing the strength and flexibility of the shoulder.

Wedges and Short Irons - At week 13, I went to the local driving range that had soft mats. Prior to this week, I had inspected the mats at several driving ranges to find a soft mat that I thought would not induce any additional stresses into my arm or shoulder from one-quarter or one-half swings. I limited my swings to one-quarter swings for approximately two weeks to ensure I was not causing any physical problems. This provided an excellent time for learning and feeling slow, smooth swings. I also focused on clubface positions while swinging through the impact point.

For the first couple of weeks I only used the sand wedge and the pitching wedge for practice sessions. This controlled my swings and focused my attention on one goal at each session. I started to use half swings at week 15 with very slow swings. I worked to ensure I would only sweep through the impact point and not hit into the mat. It is very important to me to become a sweeper rather than hit into the back of the ball. My shoulder condition is far too important to damage it attempting to increase backspin or flight height on the ball.

Each week from week 13 through week 22, I would subdivide practice days into separate and distinct practice sessions. Each session would have a singular focus and purpose such as putting accuracy, chip distance and accuracy, or wedge distance control and directional accuracy. Swing feel, backswing and forward swing control, shot distance control, and repeatability started to become consistent. Wow, it was all coming together with one-quarter and one-half swings.

Post Surgery Weeks

Operation 3-26-08

Activity	0 - 2	3 - 4	5 - 6	7 - 8	9 - 10	11 - 12	13 - 14	15 - 16	17 - 18	19 - 20	21 - 22	23 - 24
Physical Therapy Activity												
Dr. Dreese Visit		Dr=4-29		Dr=5-27			Dr=6-24				Dr=8-26	
Passive ROM Exercises												
Wall Walk												
Arm Lifts, Isometrics, Thera-band												
Scapular Strengthening												
Rotator Cuff Strengthening												
Plyometric Activities												
		W4=4-23		W6=5-7		W11=6-11		W16=7-16			W22=8-27	

Activity	0 - 2	3 - 4	5 - 6	7 - 8	9 - 10	11 - 12	13 - 14	15 - 16	17 - 18	19 - 20	21 - 22	23 - 24
Golf Swing Rehabilitation				≤ 1/4 Swing			≤ Half Swing			≤ 3/4 Swing		
Practice Green												
Putting												
Chipping												
Pitching												
Driving Range [Soft Mat / Tees]												
Wedges [PW & LW]												
Short Irons [7 - 9]												
Hybrids [4 - 6]												
Fairway Woods [3 - 7]												
Driver												

Initiate Golf Play 9/10/2008
Notes Regarding **1st Six Months** of Golf Play
1. Use NO More than 3/4 Swing for all shots
2. Use Wooden Tees for all Tee shots, Fairway, Rough, and Wedge shots
3. No bunker shots [Tee Ball Outside Bunker in Rough]

Illustration No.1: Recovery Period and Skills Development Schedule

Hybrids and Fairway Metals – With the increased flexibility and strength at week 16, the physical therapists recommended that I could start full swings based on my rehab progress. I was not ready for the full-swing shot, so I continued with the half swing when I moved up to the hybrid and fairway metals. Again, I started with slow swings to sweep through the impact point. This half swing shot-making increased my accuracy and confidence in controlling distance.

At week 20, I increased my backswing to three-quarters. I was very pleased with the direction and ball flight. My distance was lacking at first, and I was concerned, but I got over it quickly when I realized my strength and flexibility were still limited.

Take It to the Course – Week 17 was a good week. I went to the course with some friends. They played 18 holes, I followed them around the course, and I enjoyed it. At approximately 100 yards, I would place a ball on a tee and make a half shot into the green with a short iron. I was very pleased I hit almost every green. My friends were very surprised with my shot accuracy, chipping and putting. I birdied all the par fours and eagled half of the par fives.

At week 22, I started to play a full round. I used the three-wood for most tee shots. I did not bring the driver to the course. I was very pleased with my scores and enjoyed getting out with friends.

The big dog was introduced back into the game at week 25. I still am working to increase strength, and eventually distance will return. If it does not I will adapt and be happy I can still play after major surgery.

Important Rules:

The full swing will be limited to quarter swings during most of the rehabilitation effort.

A slow half swing may be introduced at ~ week 13 or when shoulder and back strength allows it.

For the first six months of golf play all shots will be teed above the ground to protect the

shoulder. [Tee area, fairway, and first cut]

No shots will be played out of a fairway or green side bunker; hand wedges will be employed, for at least six months after initiating golf play.

Practice

Practice is essential while developing new skills in any endeavor. Each practice session must be sensible and have a clear and simple purpose with an obtainable objective. There is a significant amount of practice suggested to develop the shot skills and establish a solid golf foundation. Practice should not be viewed as drudgery but as an opportunity to learn new skills. Practicing golf techniques is an experience in creativity, and when new skills are learned, confidence increases along with self-esteem.

Most of these practice sessions can be exercised while the shoulder is recovering from the trauma of surgery. Do not over practice; it will hurt your shoulder and possibly frustrate you because of swing limitations. Hitting golf balls long and straight is more the result of core rotation speed and body flexibility than brute strength. Practice taking the club back slow and smoothly, and forward through impact effortlessly. Perhaps you will be as surprised as I was with how well the ball flies with a good swing balance and tempo. Use impact tape to validate swing improvements and consistency.

Quality practice does make quality skills. Each time you go to the practice range, you should have a clear plan, one swing thought, and one goal for that session. This process should help you focus. Practicing in a methodical manner produces noticeable results. Plan that every practice shot should have a target alignment reference, and a precise alignment, stance, posture, and grip. Practicing mindfully with the intent to learn something new and to sense the swing tempo and swing balance will create a solid foundation. Take two practice swings to feel the shot prior to executing each shot.

Add stretching after strengthening the shoulders, arms, hips, legs, and back through the PT exercises and acquiring shot skills. Before starting each practice session do stretching moves to loosen joints, muscles, hands, arms, and legs. Rotate the shoulders and arms slowly through a moderate range of motion for a couple of minutes. Swing two clubs or a weighted club very slowly as quarter and then half swings to loosen the back prior to initiating any practice shots.

Practice recovery shots with the wedges and short irons from poor lies, side hill lies, and pitches over green side bunkers. On the range, select targets at different distances to flags to practice hitting targets. Mix up the shot order to exercise the mind as well as the body.

Practice Facilities

Most golf facilities have limited practice areas. There are very few public short-game practice greens to chip or pitch some shots. Very few facilities have bunkers or short shot areas with markers every five yards to 50 yards and/or every ten yards up to 100 yards. With limited facilities and limited practice time, average golfers have a very hard time improving their short-game skills. If a practice facility is not accessible to you, create a temporary practice field at your local common area or school. Purchase some inexpensive small soccer field cones and lay them at five-yard intervals to measure chip, pitch, and short-iron shot fly distances during practice sessions.

Record Keeping

Maintain a record book detailing all development steps and practice sessions. Record your accomplishments and setbacks so progress can be evaluated. Routinely review the practice log to identify areas needing extra effort to meet practice objectives and plan goals. Set up a simple spreadsheet to track [visualize] progress of each element [putts, chips, wedges, short irons, hybrids, fairway metals]. Record keeping is as important as the practice session. Collecting shot information during post-surgery rehabilitation provides a means to stay interested in the practice sessions and to visualize the improvements accomplished during this period.

Many instructors would have you adjusting swing speeds, changing hand positions, altering backswing distances, and moving ball positions in your setup to vary short shot flights and distances. I recommend a far simpler system of one hand position and two backswing distances.

How much data collection is too much? Well, if you were to collect shot data for two to three hand positions on the grip and two to three backswing positions, several ball positions, and several swing tempos, it would be overwhelming. This could be 18 data points for each club for each chip and for each pitch shot. It could be another 18 data points for each short-iron shot and nine data points for each hybrid and fairway metal shot. Do you have a headache? It could be 92 to 252 distance and roll records. Just measuring and recording this amount of data would probably make an average geek tired. Unless you have a severe case of "the nerdy geek," this seems like information overload.

Perhaps one should keep it interesting, simple, and achievable by starting with one hand position for chips and pitches [bottom of grip] and one hand position for short irons, hybrids, and fairway metals [top/normal]. Initially the backswing positions should also be limited to two positions for all clubs with one swing tempo and one ball position. This would then reduce the data points to an amount less nerdy of two per club per shot type or 46 for all shot types per club set. For most of us average golfers, this number is enough.

The most important set of shot skills are the ones you have confidence in during a round. If you have confidence with one club for chip shots and one club for pitch shots, then stay with the two clubs. Do not overcomplicate your learning or the ability to reach your goals. Feeling shots really means having confidence with a soft grip and smooth swing. Do not try to steer the club or clubface; our hands are not that fast. The ball makes contact with the club for less than 300 microseconds.

After collecting shot fly and roll distances for the chip and pitch shots, create simple typed record sheets and reduce them to a size that can be glued to a business card. This business card could have chip shot data on one side and pitch shot data on the other side. Laminate the card and you will have your own personal caddy. You could also make a record of short-iron shot data, hybrid shot, and fairway metal shot data. This could provide much needed information regarding your average carry distances for second or third shots to greens and perhaps lower scores.

Simple scorecard record keeping methods during rounds to self-assess intrinsic golf skills during a specific round and during a season will be addressed later in this document.

Summary

Understanding how adjustments to grip position, ball position, and setup can vary shot length and flight dynamics is vital to achieving a low handicap. Maintaining a swing tempo and a balanced swing for all shots is essential to lowering scores and establishing a solid golf foundation.

This document emphasizes practice to achieve positive results. Following the details for each shot skill will get you very close to success. Minor adjustments may be necessary due to our physical condition. These adjustments should be the same for all shots and should become your personal setup for success.

Single-swing attribute-focused practice sessions for each specific shot skill should provide immediate results. During each practice session, concentrate on feeling soft hands, a slow swing, and the club-head performing the intended action.

Avoid practice sessions with multiple improvements and/or changes as the primary goal. Learn the specific shot execution details once through focused practice sessions; do not go into information overload or practice fatigue by overdoing the learning process. After attaining the swing and shot skills, keep practice methods, skill goals, and a development schedule clear and simple to be obtainable. A quality practice session once or twice per month should sustain a reasonable set of shot skills.

Upon learning and obtaining skills through section three and four guidance, the improvements should be solidified when swing balance and tempo are consistent throughout all shot types. Occasionally some small amount of swing tuning and experimenting should be practiced to keep the best swing functioning successfully. Conduct this fine-tuning at a practice facility and not on the course.

SECTION THREE

Golf Skill Guidance

I believe this sequence of golf shot skill development should be the approach to all beginning or rehabilitation golf instruction. If a person learns the importance of shot-making on the green and around the green, scoring and enjoyment will be maximized early. These two important elements are closely linked by placing short shots on the green and close to the hole; these are the vital elements in a golfer's skill set.

The hybrids and fairway metals are where technology has helped the average golfer. These golf clubs enable moderate handicap golfers the opportunity to score par on most par-five holes. Scoring par on most par-four holes requires an ability to make solid contact with the hybrid clubs and fairway metal clubs and accurately land the ball on the green.

Only low handicap golfers should use the "big dog" driver. Most moderate to high handicap golfers [average] should use a three wood on the par-four and par-five tees. Three woods typically fly further for the high handicapper and provide more consistency off the tee. However, egos are difficult to dampen.

The bunker shot is addressed last in this document because it requires a fully functional shoulder and back to execute the greenside and fairway bunker shots.

Golf Swing Information and You

It is important to discuss the aspects of learning a golf swing before going into the nuances of each type of golf shot. After learning golf skills from sections three and four and your practice sessions, come back and read this subsection again.

There are many golf instruction books, DVDs, magazines, and info commercials describing and selling the latest swing guidance. Much of the information is good, and some of the teaching aids are satisfactory.

However, a word of caution regarding the exchange of information related to the game of golf. There are very few true fundamentals to the game of golf; there are many approaches to shot execution, playing a hole, scoring, and enjoying this great game. Fine-tuning the alignment, stance, and ball position relative to the suggestions in this guidance document is expected depending on your body type and degree of fitness.

There is only one true essential element to a golf swing, and that is the grip. Having a fundamentally sound grip is vital to acquiring shot success and game enjoyment. Learning how to grip a golf club so that wrist hinging, swing tempo, and a square clubface position at impact feels natural is most important. **Once the grip is understood and comfortable and it permits a free-flowing swing, do not ever change it. If it works, do not fix it.**

Some instructions will suggest changing the grip; usually the instructor means change the position of the clubface, relative to ball path, or shaft length to execute a shot. Rotating the club shaft (clubface) relative to the ball path during setup or adjusting the shaft length is necessary for shot-making. The fundamental grip (hands) and firmness should remain the same for all shots. The natural ability to return a clubface smoothly through the impact position is key to all quality shots.

Many instructors will explain in great detail how to position your feet, bend your knees, tilt your upper torso, and hang your arms in a shot setup. Most of the information is fundamentally sound for a golfer of reasonable fitness. Most of us are flexibility, strength, height, or body shape challenged. We must understand how to adjust the setup or swing guidance to fit our current state of fitness. Knowing where your intrinsic swing bottom position is relative to your feet and torso is essential for shot consistency. Acknowledging flexibility and strength limitations is important to club selection and swing dynamics.

For some of us the lack of flexibility may require the ball to be played slightly back. For others an open stance may be necessary if the clubface is delayed by hip problems. Others may have to play a fade due to core rotation limitations. These refinements, once identified and adjusted as necessary, should be considered as your setup and swing baseline unless something changes in your level of fitness.

Find Your Swing

The best method to find your ideal swing is to practice slow, smooth swings with equal distance in the back and forward directions. Start with quarter or half swings, whichever is most comfortable, to get a feel for how a swinging club head feels. Locate the bottom of your swing path and note its position relative to your feet. The swing bottom will vary depending on how much the width of your stance changes for quarter, half, and three-quarter swings.

Next set up with a square alignment and a stance per the full-swing guidance within this document, and hit some balls with a slow, smooth swing. Are you surprised how far the ball flies with a smooth, flexible swing? Note which direction the ball flies; if it flies to the left or right, a minor setup change may be necessary. Most setup instructions do not account for flexibility and strength constraints and body types.

For most of us, slight alignment changes relative to ball position are necessary to ensure a smooth swing and a square clubface through the impact zone. The Laws of the Golf Swing, by Adams, Tomasi, and Suttie, is a very good book that addresses golf swing laws and body types.

Most golf books talk about HITTING the ball and swinging hard into the impact zone. Most of us cannot control our swing sufficiently to swing hard or fast. The absolute most important elements of a swing are tempo, balance, and clubface position at impact. Learning how to make quality swings with a relatively moderate swing speed will initiate the process of building and understanding your intrinsic swing tempo. Equalizing the back and forward swing distances with a good weight shift will give your swing balance. Setting up with a square clubface and seeing your smooth swing send the ball slightly off track provides feedback on your setup, swing dynamics, and fitness. Some minor adjustment to clubface position and/or ball position may be necessary to acquire a repeatable and predictable ball flight. Once adjustments are identified and validated through practice, do not look for more things to change.

Skill Set Priorities

The two most essential elements in a golfer's skill set are a consistent and confident short game and a balanced full swing. 1) A short-game skill set with known and repeatable chip and pitch shots and with quarter and half swing short-iron shots is vital. 2) A balanced swing with a soft grip pressure, a smooth tempo, and equal distance back and forward motion is irreplaceable. These two elements are the foundation for a quality skill set and game. Mental and physical elements are important to establish a foundation with these essential elements. Use of the balanced swing with good tempo for all clubs will increase the "greens in regulation" (GIR) and par saves throughout every round.

Swing Key Points

Where should I summarize the key points related to shot-making and swing dynamics that will be presented in this section? I believe it is important to communicate in a summary manner the essentials of a quality golf swing for multiple types of shots. As you examine, learn, and practice the detailed shot execution steps described in this document, it is very important to understand that the golf swing can and should be thought of as a smooth and balanced movement of the arms, legs, and torso. Let us look at the key principles of a balanced and effective swing that will be addressed in learning specific golf shots.

Most of these principles are true for all golf shots.

Setup

- A correct grip is a golf fundamental necessity.
- Always align the clubface lines perpendicular to a near-field target at setup.

Notes: A near-field target is an object, divot, weed, or bare spot several feet in front of the ball and along the target line.

This near-field object is used to accurately align the clubface with the target line at setup.

This is much more reliable than attempting to align the clubface with the far-field target.

Backswing

- Start the club moving back after a small forward press toward the target.
- A low, slow, straight [sweep the grass] start to the backswing leads to a longer swing arc.
- Rotate only the shoulder for the first foot of the backswing. Delay the hip turn to build [coiled core] some swing torque.
- Average golfers should limit their backswings to a three-quarter position to manage a balanced swing with no loss of effectiveness.

Forward Swing

- Sweep the club forward and down on a slight inside track toward the back of the ball, impact point.
- Initiate the downswing by shifting weight and rotating the hips forward, coiled core; the arms and club will follow the core.
- An unhurried start to the downswing provides for a gradual increase in swing speed through the impact area without disturbing swing tempo or swing balance.
- Bring the back elbow close to your side at the start of the downswing.
- Stay behind the ball; keep the forward ear

behind the ball through impact.

- Swing the club smoothly and freely through the ball position, not at the ball position.
- Your hands will naturally tighten on the downswing. Try not to grip the club too tight [do not choke the chicken] on the downswing. It eliminates wrist flexibility.
- The wrist will automatically unhinge and the hands should rotate through the impact zone naturally. Do not try to manipulate the clubface.

Note: During the swing, I sometimes think the following to synchronize my swings. Back — "Slowly Turn Shoulders" and Forward — "Shift Forward, Turn Hips."

Finish

- Finish the swing with your belly button pointing at your intended target.
- Hands should finish high and next to your head.

Swing Fundamentals

- Swing balance is necessary for success.
- A smooth swing with relaxed muscles is

essential for successful shot execution.

- Swing at 80% of full power for maximum distance and accuracy.
- The rotated core [coiled] is the swing engine.
- Do not sway during the swing. Back knee should be leaning toward ball during the backswing.
- Balance Swing – Forward swing distance and speed should match backswing distance and speed.
- Tempo – Keep swing smooth, shot distance controlled by swing tempo and backswing distance
- Eyes – Keep eyes looking at the back of the ball.
- Ball Flight – Height of shot controlled by swing distance after impact.

Game

- Target – Keep focused on target; ignore hazards and bunkers. Use sufficient club to clear hazards with margin.
- Focus – Keep focused on the positive aspects of your shot skills and game.
- Approach Ball on Green – Walk toward ball with a clear view of the green slopes and

probable ball roll to understand and factor green influences into the putt.

Swing Modification and Shot Control

Sometimes the swing timing and feel are just not there for specific clubs. This will happen more often as we become more seasoned in life. Some clubs feel good and the shot results are acceptable; as changes occur to our flexibility and strength, some clubs become awkward to swing. I assume you are like most golfers and have an iron, a hybrid, and a fairway metal that are your feel-good clubs.

When this swing awkwardness occurs, take your favorite iron, hybrid, and/or fairway metal and make some practice swings and shots at the driving range. When the swing timing, feel, and balance and shot results are where you want them with your favorite club, note where your hand position is on your favorite club relative to the distance from the club head. Change clubs to the one with the problem and place your hands on the troubled club at the same location relative to distance from the club head. This should provide a similar swing feel as your favorite club when you make some practice swings. Keep your hands at this length and make some practice shots. The shot control and feel should be very similar to your favorite club. WOW, I feel good again with my clubs and shots.

This slight modification to the shaft length, with the grip in a lower position, becomes necessary to reacquire a quality swing and better shot control as we become more seasoned. I believe this was the concept, shorter shaft lengths, behind the success of the "the club" several years ago. The hybrids provide improved ball flight over the irons with the same club loft because of changes in club head weight distribution.

A small amount of loss in fly distance may occur, or you may actually increase your shot distance, keep it in the short grass, and improve your game satisfaction. With this adjustment, you may have to give your playing partner a couple of strokes after he/she notices your improvement. My last point with regard to regaining shot control is that the hand position adjustment is less costly than purchasing a new set of clubs and being disappointed by the results.

Subsection Organization

To summarize, each shot guidance subsection is structured to form a solid golf foundation from the green, through the fairway, and then back to the tee area. The subsections are grouped as On the Green; Around the Green; Short Shots; Hybrids and Fairway Metals; the Big Dog; and finally Bunker Shots.

On the Green

Putting

The primary objectives for the putting stroke are to improve the consistency with returning a square putter face to the ball and to reduce the putts per round to < 32.

Putting Technique

Grip – Place hands on the club with the V of each hand pointing to its ear. Having the hands in opposition restricts, not eliminates, the hinging of the wrist's movement. Ensure the thumbs are on top of the club and point down the shaft. The grip should be soft and relaxed.

Stance – Position your eyes on a line directly over the ball or just to the inside of it. Allow a normal stroke that moves back on a slight inside path and returns to a square face through impact. Keep good balance with the weight evenly distributed [50 – 50]. The feet are usually 8 to 12 inches apart at the insides of the heels.

Ball Position – Somewhere between the left instep and the heel, it depends on stance width. Place the ball on the green [after cleaning] with the ball number in the middle of the back. Swing the putter face into the ball number.

Stroke – Should be a smooth pendulum type stroke with only the shoulders moving [arms and hands follow shoulders]. Avoid any form of wrist hinge; take the putter back low and slow to the length required for the putt distance. Gradually accelerate the putter head through the ball on the forward stroke and match swing length at both ends of the swing [distance back and forward].

Vision – Shoulders rock back and forward smoothly like a pendulum to execute the shot; keep the clubface square to target line throughout stroke.

Steady Head and Eyes – If you move your head or eyes, your shoulder will also move, which will move the shot off line. After aligning yourself relative to the putt line, keep your eyes focused on the ball number during the putter stroke. Look at the hole after the putter has passed through the contact point.

Note: The most important elements of good

putting are a comfortable stance and a swing path that returns a square putter face to the intended initial putt path.

Putting Practice

Use a putting practice area to:

1. Learn a consistent setup stance that allows the putter face to return to a square position as the putter passes through the ball position.
2. Practice one-foot through six-foot putts with your most comfortable setup and stroke.
3. Practice until seven out of ten putts < three feet on a smooth, level practice surface are holed.
4. Limit each practice session to one-half hour.

Home Putter Alignment Suggestion

If you do not have a putting mat, then the following should help.

- Use a one-foot length of masking tape or duct tape. Place it on the floor or carpet in a straight line.

- Mark a line perpendicular to the tape length near the mid length of the tape.
- See if your putter has an alignment line on the top of the putter head. If not, mark an alignment point on the top of the putter head at the mid length point with a Sharpie.
- Use the edge of the tape as a target line.
- Align yourself and the putter face relative to the tape's edge [target line]. Practice putting strokes while keeping the center of the putter head on the tape edge.
- You should keep the putter face perpendicular to the target line for approximately two inches before the ball contact point and two inches after the ball contact point.
- Adjust your putting stance [width, position to ball, openness or closeness] until you have a comfortable and repeatable stroke through the ball contact point.
- Practice with a ball to see if your stroke changes with the presence of a ball.
- Once you have achieved this setup position with stroke consistency, keep it until your physical condition changes.
- Limit practice sessions to avoid backaches

from putting stance.

Putter Contact Point Check

Sometimes putter alignment marks are not at the optimum point for repeatable straight putts. Using the Home Putter Alignment Suggestion setup:

- Hold the putter very softly in your hands and putt several balls.
- Change the position of the ball relative to putter face length approximately one-half inch after two or three putts at each position.
- You should be able to find the ball/clubface position where the clubface does not turn/twist after contacting the ball.
- Mark this position as the true contact point for your putter.
- Repeat several putts to ensure clubface does not twist.

Putting Green

1. Take refined putting technique to a practice green. Practice making putts to reacquire the feel of the green. Limit initial practice to < one hour.

2. On practice green, make six of ten three-foot putts.

3. On practice green, level area, practice lag putts to following standard for first level [four month] and second level [eight month] short-term goals; limit practice session to one hour.

   a. 10 foot to within one foot of hole [90%] and [100%]

   b. 20 foot to within two feet of hole [80%] and [90%]

   c. > 30 foot to within three feet of hole [70%] and [90%]

Routine Putting Practice

Practice putting for at least 20 minutes per week to sustain the achieved putting skill. Never practice without an achievable goal [five of ten three-foot putts holed and three of ten six-foot putts holed].

Around the Green

Short Shot Options and Variations

What is the difference between a chip shot and a pitch shot? With endless golf tips there are endless descriptions of technique and purpose.

Chip Shot

- A chip shot flies low for a short distance with a longer roll distance to the hole.
- Chip shots are most effective from the greenside fringe and closely cut fairway near the putting surface.
- Chip shots are executed without any wrist hinging.

Pitch Shot

- Pitch shots fly high for a short distance with little ball roll after landing.
- Pitch shots are short shots with lots of early wrist hinging to fly the ball high and land softly.
- Pitch shots are typically used when the ball needs to fly over a hazard or from thick grass to the green with little roll.
- Wedges and short irons have shaft lengths

nearly the same, so one's stance and ball position are essentially the same for all pitch shots.

While developing new or revising previous short-game shot skills, know your limitations. Here are a few of the endless tips to building a short shot arsenal.

- Varying swing tempo [difficult to master] to alter shot length,
- Changing the hand position on the grip in one-inch increments [small shot length differences] to alter shot length,
- Changes to stance width and backswing length to alter shot length, and
- Ball position changes [difficult to master] to alter flight height.

If one were to build a skill set with all these variables and with three to four wedges, the possibilities [> 128 shots] would give a pro caddy a headache. I believe that one should start with limited options and a simple set of variables and learn them through multiple hours of purposeful practice. This alone would cause a significant improvement for most average golfers. The suggestions in this document for chip and pitch shots are limited to the following.

- Three wedges [LW, SW, PW]
- One hand position on a grip [bottom]
- One swing tempo
- One ball position [big toe of back foot]
- Chips – Two backswing positions for hands [7:30 & 9:00]
  - 7:30 = halfway between setup position and 9:00 position
  - Pitches – Two backswings [$\frac{1}{4}$, $\frac{1}{2}$]
  - One-quarter with partial hinge and half with full hinge

This reduces the chip shot and the pitch shot options to six each. This seems much more manageable. The most important element of short-game shots is having some that you have confidence in for reducing a round's score.

Chip Shot

Chipping with success is essential to lowering one's score. Establishing a sound chip shot skill will improve one's score immediately. Some golfers chip with only one club, and others chip with multiple clubs. If you use one club, you must have an excellent feel for the shot and a variable swing tempo to manage the various shot distances. If you use multiple clubs, the swing tempo can remain the same for each club and let the difference in clubface loft change the shot distance.

Chip Shot Objectives

Develop repeatable chip shot technique that is accurate and consistent at specific distances. Learn specific chip lengths for shots where hands go back with no wrist hinge to club head positions of 7:30 and 9:00 on backswings with LW, SW, PW, and 9I.

Chipping Key Points

- The most effective chip shot is a low shot to get the ball on the putting surface as soon as possible and rolling smoothly toward the hole.
- Accuracy and distance control are vital factors to quality shots.
- Match the backswing and forward swing distances.
- Establish one stance and grip position with hands ahead of ball for all chips.

- Keep weight 70% on forward leg; keep upper body leaning forward throughout swing.
- Keep arms close to chest throughout swing, rock shoulders to execute shot; maintain consistent swing tempo.
- Learn to aim and set up to a specific near-field target.

Ball Flight

Low Ball Flight – Use Eight Iron

Moderately High Ball Flight – Use PW or Nine Iron, ball positioned at back foot big toe

High Ball Flight – Use LW or SW, ball positioned at back foot big toe

Ball Lie

Hot Shot – Ball sitting up on top of grass will come off easily and travel far

Flyer Shot – Ball sits down slightly with grass interference with clubface at impact; ball will come out quickly with a wedge

Short Shot – Ball sitting well below grass top;

must be dug out with SW or LW

Grip – Hold the club with a standard club grip, grip down to bottom of grip for control, keep your hands soft and firm, keep grip ahead of clubface, and no wrist hinging during the stroke.

Stance – Take a narrow stance open to target at approximately 30 to 40 degrees, chip with the ball back in your stance, position ball even with your back big toe, bend the knees, keep the back straight, no shoulder slouch, set your weight [~70%] on your left side, and do not move legs during shot.

Stroke – Keep upper arms close to chest throughout the swing and let the back and shoulders do the work; move the club back by rocking shoulders backward with a small turn of the body and no wrist action. Keep top of the shaft ahead of the club head through impact; visualize a paintbrush moving smoothly and squarely back and forward through the impact point. Match both ends of the swing; the distance toward the target should match the backswing distance.

Vision – Shoulders rock back and forward like a pendulum to execute the shot; the clubface looks like a three-inch paintbrush painting a straight swath along the target line.

> **Notes: If you move your head or eyes, your shoulder will also move, which will move the shot off line.**

Do not attempt to vary swing speed to alter shot distance.

Hybrid Chip

Grip down on the shaft an inch or two for added control; feet should be six to eight inches apart at the heels, and weight should be 70% on forward foot. Set the shaft angle upright and forward with the butt end pointing toward your left pocket; the ball should be in middle of stance.

- Keep your shoulders square to the target; make an extended putting motion into the ball, and
- The hands and wrists should remain still; ball will come out low with little spin, and it should roll rather far. **Practice.**

Club Selection

Use a less lofted club [8I] for chips two feet or less from putting surface and pin is close to ball position. Use a lob or sand wedge when the ball is several yards off the green and pin is close to the green edge. Use best club to limit backswing and get the ball to the hole. If fringe grass is more than two inches high, use a lofted wedge. It is best to learn to chip with a three-club set—do not make it complicated. Document chip distances after achieving shot confidence. Here are advertised shot fly/roll guidelines.

Club	Fly Distance	Ground Roll
LW	3/4	1/4
SW	2/3	1/3
PW	1/2	1/2
9I	1/3	2/3
8I	1/4	3/4

Chipping Practice

1. Learn a consistent grip and setup stance that allows the clubface to return to a square position as the face passes through the ball.
2. Practice until most chip strokes travel on a straight line toward the desired target.

3. Limit each practice session to one hour.
4. Chip Shot Skills
   a. Learn specific chip shots where hands go back with no wrist hinge to club head positions of 7:30 and 9:00 with LW, SW, PW, and 9I.
   b. Learn specific chip distances [fly and roll] for shots from a tight lie [short grass].
   c. Take two practice swings before hitting each chip shot.
   d. Practice until chip shot is repeatable to meet goals.
5. Practice chip shots to following standard for first level [four months] and second level [eight months] short-term goals; limit each practice session to one hour.
   a. < 10 foot to within one foot of hole [80%] and [90%]
   b. 5 – 20 yards to within three feet of hole [70%] and [80%]
   c. 20 – 30 yards to within six feet of hole [60%] and [70%]

Important: Practice chipping from smooth, close cut grass to get the feel for the shots.

Save Shot Information

After determining your average shot distances [Fly / Roll End] record and store the yardage information for easy retrieval in a table similar to table 3.1, the Chip Shot Record.

Routine Chipping Practice

Practice chipping for at least 15 minutes per week to sustain the achieved chipping skill. Never practice without specific targets and achievable goals. Take two practice strokes for every chip shot [make six of ten high-quality chip shots].

Table 3.1: Chip Shot Record

Club	Grip Position	Backswing	Fly / Roll
LW	Bottom	8:00	5/9
LW	Bottom	9:00	10/13
SW	Bottom	8:00	5/10
SW	Bottom	9:00	10/15
PW	Bottom	8:00	8/16
PW	Bottom	9:00	18/26
9I	Bottom	8:00	10/20
9I	Bottom	9:00	16/34
8I	Bottom	8:00	14/28
8I	Bottom	9:00	16/32

Pitch Shot

Having the confidence to pitch over a hazard and land the ball close to the hole will win many a hole. Having the ability to open the wedge face and flop a pitch shot to a pin cut close to the edge of the green will make many rounds enjoyable.

Shot Objectives

Improve pitch shot accuracy and consistency to increase up and down percentage to > 50%. Improve percent of pitch shots reaching within three yards of hole. Establish consistent pitch skill.

Pitching Technique

A pitch shot is a high short shot, within 60 yards, to a green with little roll on the green. Accuracy and distance control are vital factors of quality shots. Match the ends of the swing, backswing and forward swing. Establish one stance and grip for all pitch shots. Learn to aim at a specific target.

What is the difference between a pitch shot and a short-iron shot? In a pitch shot the wrist hinges quickly and the swing tempo is slow and smooth. In a short-iron shot the wrist hinge and swing tempo are the same as in a full swing.

Grip – Hands should always be placed on the club so that the V's formed by the thumb and index finger of each hand should point between the golfer's back ear and shoulder. Do not reach; keep the arms and shoulders relaxed at address and during the swing. Choke down on the grip to shorten backswing and increase shot control. Ensure the grip pressure is soft and relaxed throughout the swing and that the lower palm is against the top thumb.

Stance – Bend at the hips to reach the ball with knees bent, keep back straight, no shoulder slouch. Keep upper forward arm close to chest throughout the swing. Weight should be distributed 70% forward and 30% back, and stand with your front foot off the target line by three to four inches and flared open 30 degrees; the feet should be positioned for good balance. Narrow the width for $\frac{1}{4}$ swings, and slightly wider for $\frac{1}{2}$ swings. Shoulders should be on line to target, and hands should be forward of the ball.

Ball Position – Should be two inches forward of

back foot, which should be the bottom of your swing. Ensure ball position is at the bottom of your swing.

Stroke – Match both ends of the swing; the swing distance toward the target should match the backswing distance. The length of backswing determines the shot distance. The hands should hinge very early in backswing and unhinge through the ball. Clubface should point toward the target throughout the entire swing [no rotation], and you want the pitch to fly high and land softly with a little roll to the hole.

Vision – Shoulders rock back and forward like a pendulum, wrists hinge quickly, clubface is square to target line at impact, and hands finish high.

Club Selection – Club loft determines the height of the pitch shot—open the face for a flop shot. Do not attempt a shot you have not practiced, and use the best club to limit the backswing and get the ball on the green and close to the hole.

Pitch Shot Practice

Driving Range

1. Practice using a slow, smooth swing with soft hands.
2. Practice returning a square face through the ball. Ensure club is making solid/center contact.
3. Practice matching the swing speed in the backward and forward directions.
4. Practice $\frac{1}{4}$ and $\frac{1}{2}$ swings with hands at the bottom and at the top of the grip to vary shot distance.
5. Practice using yardage or other markers as targets.
6. Practice until the swing is comfortable and repeatable with wedges and short irons.
7. Practice pitch shots of 10, 20, 30, 40, and 50 yards with LW, PW, and SW.
8. At the end of a practice session see if you can hit one shot to each distance defined in step 7.
9. After becoming proficient with these shots, record fly and roll distances for each club in a table similar to Table 3.2.

Practice Green

1. Practice making short pitches to acquire a feel for the shot. Limit practice sessions to one hour.
2. On the green, practice until five of ten pitches from 10 to 20 yards are within three feet of hole. Limit practice sessions to one hour.
3. Practice pitch shots from tight lies [fairways] of 10, 20, 30, 40, and 50 yards.
4. Practice pitch shots from greenside areas with moderate grass level [two to three inches] of 10, 20, 30, 40, and 50 yards.
5. Pitch Shot Skills
    a. Learn specific pitch distances where hands go back for $\frac{1}{4}$ and $\frac{1}{2}$ backswings with LW, SW, and PW.
    b. Take two practice swings before each pitch shot.
    c. Practice until pitch shot can be repeated 50% of time.
6. On practice green, practice pitch shots to following standard for first level [four month] and second level [eight month] short-term goals; limit practice session to one hour.

    a. 10 yards to within one yard of hole [50%] and [70%]

    b. 20 yards to within three yards of hole [50%] and [70%]

    c. 30 yards to within five yards of hole [50%] and [70%]

Save Shot Information

After determining your average shot distances, record and store the information for easy retrieval in a table similar to table 3.2.

Table No. 3.2: Pitch Shot Record

Club	Grip	Backswing	Fly/Roll
LW	Bottom	Quarter	10/14
LW	Bottom	Half	18/20
SW	Bottom	Quarter	11/17
SW	Bottom	Half	15/20
PW	Bottom	Quarter	20/32
PW	Bottom	Half	34/36
9I	Bottom	Quarter	22/32
9I	Bottom	Half	26/38

Routine Pitching Practice

Practice pitching for at least 20 minutes per week to sustain the achieved pitching skill. Never practice without specific targets and achievable goals. Take two practice swings before each pitch shot [make seven of ten high-quality pitch shots].

Short Shots

Wedges and Short Irons

Complementing a solid chip and pitch skill set with the ability to put a ball in the middle of the green from anywhere within 100 yards will enable you to save many pars and lower that handicap. Having confidence to execute a quarter or half swing shot when necessary will invigorate anyone's round.

Shot Objectives

Establish wedge shot accuracy and consistency to reach greens and be within five yards of target 70%. Establish consistent shot skill with PW, SW, 9I, and 8I. Soften grip pressure and improve swing tempo.

Technique

One of the most important elements of accurate short shots is making the upper body coil and shift the weight to the back foot. The swing center should be behind the ball at the completion of the backswing. The swing center shifts to above the ball at impact and over to the forward foot at the completion of the swing.

Accuracy and distance control are vital factors to quality short shots. A wedge or short-iron shot is simply a shortened version of a full swing. Match the swing distances, backswing and forward swing. Establish one stance and grip for all wedge and short-iron shots. Learn to aim at a specific target.

Grip – Hands should always be placed on the club so that the V's formed by the thumb and index finger of each hand point between the golfer's back ear and shoulder. Keep the arms and shoulders relaxed at address and during the swing. Ensure the grip is soft and firm at address and during the swing and that the lower palm is against the top thumb.

Stance – Arms should be relaxed and hang naturally—do not reach for the ball. Bend from the hips, push your butt out past your shoe heels, and lean your torso toward the ball. Flex your knees, set your back knee slightly toward target, and keep your back straight. Stand with a forward tilt and with your back shoulder lower than your forward shoulder. Set your front foot open 30 degrees and your back foot open five degrees. Keep the upper forward arm close to your chest throughout the swing. Weight should be 50% - 50% at setup, and the outside of your feet should be spread apart to a distance equal to the inside shoulder width.

Ball Position – Should be slightly behind the middle of the stance [zipper], which should be the bottom of your swing. Ensure ball position is at the bottom of your swing.

Stroke – Normally it should be a half or three-quarter swing. Match both ends of the swing; the swing distance toward the target should match the backswing distance, and the hands should hinge, unhinge, and rotate freely as with a normal full shot.

Vision – Slow, smooth backswing with a coiled core, hips start an unhurried forward swing through impact area, ball flies high toward target, to a high finish looking at the target.

Club Selection – Club loft determines the height of the shot; do not attempt a shot you have not practiced. Use best club to limit the backswing to either a half or three-quarter swing and get the ball on the green.

Wedge and Short-iron Practice
Driving Range
1. Practice using a slow, smooth swing with soft hands.
2. Practice returning a square clubface through the ball. Ensure club is making solid/center contact.
3. Practice making short shots [swing back to 9:00 and forward to 3:00] to acquire a feel for the shots. Limit practice sessions to one hour.
4. Practice using yardage markers as targets.
5. Practice until the swing is comfortable and repeatable with wedges or short irons and with hands at the top of grip and at the bottom of the grip for $\frac{1}{4}$, $\frac{1}{2}$, and $\frac{3}{4}$ swings.
6. Short Shot Skills
   a. Learn specific shot distances for one-quarter, one-half, and three-quarter swings with SW, PW, 9I, and 8I until they are repeatable with confidence and 80% repeatability.
   b. After gaining some shot skills, set up

targets at ten-yard intervals. Try to hit five shots to each target.

c. Next, after gaining confidence with your shot skills in step b alternate one shot to front, middle, and back targets. Change clubs and targets randomly to test skills and to build confidence.

d. Take two practice swings before each shot.

e. Practice until shot repeatability meets goals.

7. Practice shots to following standard for first level [four months] and second level [eight months] short-term goals; limit practice session to one hour.

One-quarter, one-half, and three-quarter shots within five yards of hole [50%] and [70%].

Save Shot Information

After determining your average shot distances, record and store the information for easy retrieval in a table similar to table 3.3.

Table No. 3.3: Short-iron Shot Record

Club	Grip	Backswing	Distance
SW	Top	Quarter	20
SW	Top	Half	40
SW	Top	$\frac{3}{4}$	55
PW	Top	Quarter	35
PW	Top	Half	65
PW	Top	$\frac{3}{4}$	95
9I	Top	Quarter	45
9I	Top	Half	75
9I	Top	$\frac{3}{4}$	105
8I	Top	Half	85
8I	Top	$\frac{3}{4}$	125

Routine Practice

Practice pitching for at least 15 minutes per week to sustain the achieved shot skill. Never practice without specific targets and achievable goals. Take two practice swings before each shot [make six of ten high-quality shots].

Hybrid and Fairway Metal Shot Options

Hybrids can be a golfer's best tool. Hybrids can be used for chip shots and to get a wayward drive to the green or back to the fairway. A hybrid club will pass through thick grass better than an iron. This swing development plan focuses on mastering fairway and tee shots with the hybrid clubs. The hybrids have shaft lengths very similar to mid length irons; one needs to take a stance similar to a five iron. The only shot option is for a half or three-quarter swing to control shot fly distance.

The fairway metal play options are similar to the hybrid. There is more difficulty getting a fairway metal through heavy grass with the same shot accuracy of a hybrid. This swing development plan focuses on mastering fairway and tee shots with the fairway metal clubs. The fairway metals have longer shaft length than mid length irons; one needs to take a stance a little farther from the ball. The only shot option is for a half or three-quarter swing to control shot fly distance.

Hybrid Clubs

Technology has provided golf clubs that enable an

average golfer to recover from an errant tee shot. These clubs give many amateur golfers the opportunity to dig out of roughs and advance the ball toward the hole. The new club designs and materials have prolonged many a bogey golfer's interest in the game by replacing long irons with a more tolerant hybrid.

Hybrid Shot Objectives

Improve accuracy and consistency of reaching greens in regulation and establish a consistent hybrid shot skill.

Hybrid Shot Technique

Accuracy and distance control are vital factors of quality shots. A hybrid shot is simply a version of a full swing. Match the ends of the swing [backswing and forward swing] and establish one stance and grip for all hybrid shots. Learn to aim at a specific target.

Grip – Hands should always be placed on the club so that the V's formed by the thumb and index finger of each hand should point between the golfer's back ear and shoulder. Grip pressure should be as soft as possible at address and during the backswing. Keep the arms and shoulders relaxed at address and during the swing, and ensure the lower palm is against the top thumb.

Stance – Don't reach for the ball—arms should be relaxed and hang naturally. Bend from the hips and push your butt out past your shoe heels. Flex your knees, set your back knee slightly toward target, and keep your back straight. Stand with a forward tilt, and set your back foot open five degrees and your forward foot open 30 degrees. Keep upper forward arm close to chest throughout the swing, Weight should be 50% left, 50% right, and the outside of your feet should be spread apart to a distance equal to the inside shoulder width.

Ball Position – Should be between your forward shirt pocket and your zipper and closer to the zipper for seniors. Ensure ball position is at the bottom of your swing.

Stroke – Should be one-half or three-quarter swing, match both ends of the swing [the swing distance toward the target should match the backswing distance]. You want the back elbow to be relaxed and bend as you take the club back. Hands should hinge and unhinge and rotate freely as with a normal full shot.

Vision – Relaxed muscles, smooth swing with coiled core, an unhurried forward swing through impact area, ball flies high with a slight draw, to a high finish looking at the target.

Club Selection – Do not attempt a shot you have not practiced. Use the best club to limit the backswing to a one-half or three-quarter swing and get the ball on the green.

Hybrid Practice

Driving Range
1. Practice using a slow, smooth swing with soft hands.
2. Practice using yardage markers as targets.
3. Practice until the swing is comfortable and repeatable with hands at the top of the grip and at the bottom of the grip.
4. Practice to acquire a feel for the shot.
5. Limit practice sessions to one hour.
6. Practice returning a square face to ball.

Ensure club is making solid/center contact.

a. Learn specific shot distances for one-half and three-quarter swings with 7H, 6H, 5H, and 4H.

b. Take two practice swings before each hybrid shot.

c. Practice until shot repeatability matches goals.

7. Practice shots to the following standard for first level [four months] and second level [eight months] short-term goal; limit practice session to one hour.

8. One-half swing and three-quarter swing shots within five yards of hole [50%] and [60%].

Save Hybrid Shot Information

After determining your average shot distances, record and store the information for easy retrieval. Use a table similar to table 3.4 to record shot information.

Table No. 3.4: Hybrid Shot Record

Club	Grip	Backswing	Distance
7H	Bottom	Three-Quarter	125
7H	Top	Three-Quarter	140
6H	Bottom	Three-Quarter	135
6H	Top	Three-Quarter	150
5H	Bottom	Three-Quarter	145
5H	Top	Three-Quarter	160
4H	Bottom	Three-Quarter	155
4H	Top	Three-Quarter	170

Routine Practice

Practice hybrid shots for at least 20 minutes per week to sustain the achieved shot skill. Never practice without specific targets and achievable goals. Take two practice swings before each shot [make six of ten high-quality shots].

Fairway Metal Clubs

Technology has significantly improved the fairway metal golf clubs. These clubs, with their low weight and thin, flexible [spring-like] faces, enable an average golfer to reach long four and five pars in regulation. Selecting the proper club [3, 5, 7, and 9] with a consistently smooth tempo and balanced swing enables one to reach greens in regulation and will lower that handicap.

Fairway Meal Shot Objectives

Improve accuracy and consistency of reaching green in regulation. Establish consistent fairway metal shot skill.

Fairway Metal Shot Technique

Accuracy and distance control are vital factors of quality shots. A fairway metal shot is simply a version of a full swing. Match the ends of the swing, backswing and forward swing.

Establish one stance and grip for all fairway metal shots. Learn to aim at a specific target.

Grip Hands should always be placed on the club so that the V's formed by the thumb and index finger of each hand should point between the golfer's back ear and shoulder. Grip pressure should be as soft as possible at address and during the backswing. Keep the arms and shoulders relaxed at address and during the swing. Ensure the back palm is against the top thumb.

Stance Don't reach for the ball—arms should be relaxed and hang naturally. Bend from the hips and push your butt out past your shoe heels. Flex your knees, set your back knee slightly toward target, and keep your back straight. Stand with a forward tilt and with your back foot open five to ten degrees and your forward foot open 20 to 30 degrees. Keep upper forward arm close to chest throughout the swing. Weight should be 50% left, 50% right, and the outside of your feet should be separated by the same distance as your inside shoulder width.

Ball Position Should be at or slightly behind your forward shirt pocket, which should be the bottom of your swing. Ensure ball position is at the bottom of your swing.

Stroke Should be one-half or three-quarter swing; match both ends of the swing [the swing distance toward the target should match the backswing distance]. You want the back elbow to be relaxed and bend as you take the club back. Hands should hinge, unhinge, and rotate freely as with a normal full shot.

Vision Relaxed muscles, smooth swing with coiled core, an unhurried forward swing through the impact area, ball flies high with a slight draw to a high finish looking at the target.

Club Selection Do not attempt a shot you have not practiced. Use the best club to limit the backswing to a half or three-quarter swing and get the ball on the green.

Fairway Metal Practice

Driving Range

1. Practice using a slow, smooth swing with soft hands.
2. Practice using yardage markers as targets.
3. Practice to acquire a feel for the shot.
4. Practice returning a square face to ball. Ensure club is making solid/center contact.
5. Fairway Metal Skills
   a. Learn specific shot distances for one-half and three-quarter swings with 3W, 5W, 7W, and 9W.
   b. Take two practice swings before each shot.
   c. Practice until shot repeatability meets goals.
6. Practice shots to following standard for first level [four months] and second level [eight month] short-term goals; limit practice session to one hour.
   a. Half swing and three-quarter swing shots

reach target/green [50%] and [60%].

Save Shot Information

After determining your average shot distances, record and store the information for easy retrieval in a table similar to table 3.5.

Table No. 3.5: Fairway Metal Shot Record

Club	Grip	Backswing	Distance
3W	Bottom	Three-Quarter	180
3W	Top	Three-Quarter	190
5W	Bottom	Three-Quarter	170
5W	Top	Three-Quarter	180
7W	Bottom	Three-Quarter	160
7W	Top	Three-Quarter	170
9W	Bottom	Three-Quarter	150
9W	Top	Three-Quarter	160

Routine Practice

Practice shots for at least 20 minutes per week to sustain the achieved shot skill. Never practice without specific targets and achievable goals. Take two practice swings before each shot [make six of ten high-quality shots].

The Big Dog

The driver makes many a golfer feel great when the ball flies forever off the big dog's face. Quality shots with a driver require solid balance and very good swing tempo. Technology has increased the average golfer's drive distance; this is good for the ego and one's golfing experience.

Note: Players with little time for practice or regular rounds may benefit by using a three metal from the tee.

Driver Objective

Primary Objective – Improve driver accuracy and consistency, reaching fairway target to > 75%.

Driver Shot Technique

Grip – Hands should always be placed on the club so that the V's formed by the thumb and index finger of each hand should point between the golfer's back ear and shoulder. Grip pressure should be as soft as possible at address and during the backswing. Keep the arms and shoulders relaxed at address and during the swing. Ensure the lower palm is against the top thumb.

Stance – Don't reach for the ball—arms should be relaxed and hang naturally. Bend from the hips and push your butt out past your shoe heels. Flex your knees, set your back knee slightly toward target, and keep your back straight. Stand with a forward tilt and with your back foot open five to ten degrees and your forward foot open 20 to 30 degrees. Keep upper forward arm close to chest throughout the swing. Weight should be 50% left, 50% right and the outside of both feet should be separated to match outside shoulder distance.

Ball Position – Should be between the forward instep and your forward shirt pocket, which should be the bottom of your swing. Ensure ball position is one to two inches forward of the bottom of your swing.

> **Note: You want to make ball contact as club head starts to rise after passing the swing bottom.**

Stroke – Should be a three-quarter swing; match both ends of the swing [the swing distance toward the target should match the backswing distance]. You want the back elbow to be relaxed and bend as the club goes back, and the hands should hinge and unhinge and rotate freely as with a normal full shot.

Vision – Slow, low backswing to a three-quarter position with tightly coiled core; hips rotate forward slowly as arms come from slightly inside through impact zone to a high finish looking at target.

Driver Practice at Driving Range

1. Practice using a slow, smooth swing with soft hands.
2. Practice using yardage markers as targets.
3. Practice until the swing is comfortable and repeatable with hands brought back to 10:30.
4. Practice to acquire a feel for the shot.
5. Practice returning a square face to ball. Ensure club is making solid/center contact.
6. Practice shots to following standard for first level [four months] short-term goal; limit practice session to one hour.
   a. Learn specific shot distance for three-quarter swing.
   b. Practice until shot accuracy can be repeated 70% of time

7. Practice shots to following standard for second level [eight month] intermediate goal.
   a. Learn specific shot distance for three-quarter swing.
   b. Take two practice swings before each shot.
   c. Practice until shot can be repeated 80% of time.

Save Shot Information

After determining your average shot distance, record and store the information for easy retrieval.

Routine Practice

Practice shots for at least 15 minutes per week to sustain the achieved shot skill. Never practice without specific targets and achievable goals. Take two practice swings before each shot [make six of ten high-quality shots].

Bunker Shots

Greenside Bunkers

Most of us average golfers become rather anxious when we must get our ball out of a greenside bunker and on the green. We are not talking about getting it close to the hole—just out of the bunker. Bunker shots are difficult because most of us do not have time to practice them, and most facilities do not have a bunker practice area.

Bunker Shot Overview

Bunker shot execution should include two elements. Accelerate through the shot and let your back shoulder swing toward the target. Release the open clubface into the sand at your normal swing bottom point and keep your weight [60 to 70%] on your forward foot throughout the swing. With the ball located one to two inches ahead of your normal swing bottom point at setup, it should fly out on a small mound of sand.

Greenside Bunker Shot Technique

Target – Assess where the ball should land on the green; check out the green undulations to visualize the ball rolling to the hole.

Alignment – Pick a target landing point. Your clubface should point toward the landing point at the completion of your setup. Ball will escape the bunker along the swing line, not where the clubface is pointing. The ball will fly out of the sand with sidespin; it will land on the green and roll toward where the clubface was pointing at setup.

Swing Line and Clubface Alignment – The swing line and clubface alignment will vary depending on the sand density. For soft sand, the swing line will be to the left of the target, or clubface is open to target. With wet or packed sand, your swing line will be close to matching the ball flight line, or the clubface is square to the target to allow some digging into the sand.

Grip – Place hands in the middle of the grip; open clubface to eliminate the bounce in soft sands.

Stance – Address the ball with feet set at your outside shoulder width. Set up using a forward tilted torso; establish good footing by digging feet into sand approximately one-half inch. Lean slightly toward intended target area; keep 60 to 70% of your weight on leading side. Keep your lower body still during the shot.

Note: The act of digging your feet into the sand gives you an opportunity to test the firmness of the sand.

Ball Position – Position yourself so that swing bottom is several inches behind ball.

- Ball position should be forward of swing bottom [two to three inches] for soft sand.
- Ball position should be even with swing bottom for packed or wet sand; use a pitching wedge, and
- Buried balls should be played back in your stance and dug out with SW or LW.

Stroke – Swing the shoulders to escape a bunker; use your core strength to escape the bunker. Turn your shoulders instead of lifting the shoulder. Hinge your wrist very early in the backswing; wrist should have 90-degree hinge with hands waist high. The downswing should be steeper than your normal swing; release the hands at impact to get ball airborne.

Keep lower body quiet during swing. The forward swing distance should match backswing distance.

Important: You must accelerate through the sand to get the ball airborne, finish the swing.

Place Bunker Shot Near Hole

Use your lob wedge, sand wedge, and pitching wedge, and divide a typical green into three sections.

Front Third of the Green – use your lob wedge with a square clubface and take a normal bunker swing as described above.

Middle Third of the Green – use your sand wedge; take a normal bunker swing as described above.

Back Third of the Green – use your pitching wedge; take a normal bunker swing as described above.

Note: The same swing motion with three different clubs should produce three different distances—short, medium, and

long—with the same swing speed and sand density.

Greenside Bunker Escape with a Close in Location

You have a good lie in a greenside bunker, and need a high, soft sand shot that stops on a dime.

1. Use your lob wedge. Position the ball slightly forward in your stance and move the handle of the club slightly behind your zipper to add extra loft to the clubface.
2. Spread your feet and dig both feet into the sand one-half inch for balance.
3. Swing the club with your arms and your wrists, using minimum shoulder movement.
4. Keep your upper torso tilted toward the ball and swing your arms and hands underneath your tilted torso and watch the ball fly high and land softly.

Bunker Practice

Find a bunker or sand lot for practice. Make a line, No.1, in the sand to represent a ball flight line. Make a line, No.2, in the sand to represent the club entry point, swing bottom, into the sand.

Next, you want to practice setting up to the two lines where your normal setup is aligned to the ball flight, No.1, line and the ball is two to three inches forward of the swing bottom, No.2, line.

Make practice swings with an early wrist hinge and a full release into the swing bottom line with an open clubface. Feel the club head release and notice how the sand flies along the swing path line. Next, remake the sand lines and place a ball two to three inches in front of the swing bottom line. Take practice swings with an open clubface, see where the ball lands relative to the swing line and which way it bounces. Practice to get the feel and to see where the ball goes with two to three different clubface open positions.

Vary the swing length to see the difference in ball flight distance. Also, vary the swing length and clubface position to see the effects both have on flight height and distance.

Summary

When in a greenside bunker, first determine the roll of the ball after landing on the green and the type of sand the ball is lying on which will influence target alignment. Set up to the ball with a normal swing alignment, except the ball should be two to three inches in front of the swing bottom. Dig your feet into the sand, choke up on the grip, and point clubface at the landing point. Make a three-quarter swing with an early wrist hinge, swing forward, and release the club into the sand.

Fairway Bunker

Fairway Bunker Shot Technique

1. Club Selection - Anything from a Fairway Metal, Hybrid, or Iron will work. Select one club more [5H over a 6H] than the yardage indicates for a normal fairway shot distance. The ball will normally have a low trajectory.
2. Set up for your normal full-swing shot with the following adjustments. Set your feet into the sand approximately one-half inch. Play ball slightly behind the middle of your stance. Choke down on the grip about one inch.
3. You want to strike the ball as if you do not want to take a divot. Instead, you want to make contact with the ball as cleanly as possible so that the sand does not slow up the clubface. Think of a typical fairway metal

shot where you sweep through the impact point and only touch the top of the grass.

4. You should determine whether hitting a distance shot out of a fairway bunker is the way to go. If you do not have a good shot, hit the ball out 20 or 30 yards to the fairway and give yourself a much better chance to hit the green and minimize a high score.

Note: It is nearly impossible to find a facility where you can practice escaping a fairway bunker. Perhaps the next time you are playing a practice round or just out to enjoy the day, drop one or two balls into a fairway bunker and make the shots.

SECTION FOUR

Full-Swing Guidance

T he content within this section applies to all iron, hybrid, fairway metal, and driver shots. It is very important to learn and feel the key attributes of your natural swing.

Sometimes a lack of flexibility or strength surfaces as we are warming up for the round. Feeling and/or acknowledging slight swing differences from day to day or week to week will enable you to make the fine-tuning necessary to make solid contact. It is essential to know, understand, and feel where the swing bottoms out, the physical limits of your backswing, your swing tempo, and how maintaining a balanced swing influences shot success.

This section is focused on building a solid golf swing. I emphasize the use of a three-quarter swing as a full swing. For the average golfer the three-quarter swing minimizes pulling the body out of position on the backswing. During the backswing, the grip should allow the wrist to hinge automatically when the hands reach just past waist high; a three-quarter shoulder turn should complete the swing. Relaxed arms and a soft grip will allow the wrists to naturally hinge. A coiled upper body is the primary source of power for a quality golf swing. The forward swing is initiated by a slight weight shift and the rotation of the hips toward the target, which will uncoil the upper body [swing engine]; the arms should follow this forward rotation and unhinge naturally. Executing this swing stabilizes the knee and hip vertical positions to prevent the hips from moving up or down during a swing.

Key points emphasized in this section are:

- Every shot executed during a golf round and during a practice session must have a target and a purpose.
- Every shot should be a balanced and smooth swing through the ball; forward and backswing distances should match.
- Keep grip soft [three of ten] throughout the swing; a natural wrist hinge is essential.
- A straight back should be tilted forward

from the hips, with knees bent to position the club behind the ball at setup.

- The back shoulder should be lower than the forward shoulder when addressing the ball.
- The rotation of the shoulders controls the backswing; a slight weight shift and the rotation of the hips control the downswing.
- Think sweep through the grass [target] rather than chop down at the back of the ball. Save the shoulder and wrists.
- Every club has a distance limit—change the club, not your swing force, for more distance and control.
- Quality of finish position = shot quality [tempo and balance].
- At no time should a golfer with limited flexibility or strength swing past a three-quarter position on the backswing.

Key elements of a full swing will now be addressed. I should point out that these elements apply to all one-half, three-quarter, and full swings. As you become familiar with each of these elements, do the practice suggestions until the grip, specific club position, and/or motion feels natural and effective.

Grip

1. Hands should always be placed on the club so that the V's formed by the thumb and index finger of each hand should point between the golfer's back ear and shoulder.

2. Position of the top hand at setup controls clubface at impact.

3. With an open hand, the club's grip should run from the base of the index finger to a point ~ one-half inch above the base of the little finger [check it out].

4. The lower hand wraps around the shaft, and the lower thumb pad sits firmly on top of the top thumb.

5. The top-hand thumb should be placed on the side [one o'clock] of the grip. The lower-hand thumb should be located on the side [eleven o'clock] of the grip.

6. Grip pressure should be as soft as possible [three of ten] at address and during the backswing.

7. Keep the arms and shoulders relaxed at address and during the swing.

8. Ensure the top-hand position allows wrist hinging. Top hand should have the same feeling as if you were holding a hammer. Use

a grip tool [short iron] to learn the proper feel of a good grip.

9. After achieving a grip position and firmness that allows wrist hinging and unhinging freely during your swings and it feels natural—**keep the grip**. Do not change it unless there is an injury.

Important: Without a solid grip, efforts to improve one's game will be in vain.

Note: Golfers with limited torso and arm flexibility and strength should try a stronger grip to return a square clubface at impact.

Tilt Your Torso—Don't Reach for the Ball

One should never reach for the ball. Learn the following stance, which allows for a free swing without any vertical motion of the body.

1. Turn back foot out ~ five degrees and the forward foot should be turned out ~ 20 to 30 degrees.
2. Bend from the hips and push your butt out past your shoe heels.
3. A forward-tilted torso should have a straight

back. A tilted torso facilitates a free shoulder rotation in both directions.

4. Flex your knees, and set your back knee pointing slightly toward the ball; this stabilizes the body height by maintaining some flex in the knees. It also prevents swaying during the backswing if flex is maintained.

4. Arms should be loose and hang nearly straight down to facilitate free shoulder rotation.

5. The trailing shoulder should be lower than the leading shoulder; this improves the ability of the torso to swing freely toward the target.

6. There should be no vertical motion of the hips during the swing.

Setup

Driver – The outside of the feet should be close to the outside shoulder width. If you are uncomfortable or lose swing balance, move outside of forward foot to position equal to inside of the forward shoulder. If this is not comfortable during swings and you lose swing balance, return forward foot to outside shoulder position and move the back foot to the inside position of the back shoulder.

Fairway Woods – The outside width of both feet should be positioned at the inside of the shoulders.

Hybrids – The outside of the forward foot should be at the inside of the forward shoulder, and the outside of the back foot should be approximately one inch inside the back shoulder.

Short Irons – The outside of the forward foot should be one inch inside the forward shoulder, and the outside of the back foot should be approximately one inch inside the back shoulder.

Important: The shoulders should not be closed to the target at setup.

Note: Minor adjustments to foot positions of each golfer may be necessary due to flexibility, strength, and body type issues.

Ball Position

Driver – Inside forward foot heel, check where

driver swing bottom is; ball should be ~ one to two inches forward of swing bottom position when ball is teed up.

Fairway and Hybrids – Slightly behind forward pocket, check where swing bottom is; ball should be at swing bottom position.

Short Irons – At or slightly behind zipper, check where swing bottom is; ball should be at swing bottom position.

Important: Having a repeatable swing bottom position is essential to quality shot-making. Knowing the position of the swing bottom is equally important.

Swing Plane

With a seven iron take a setup position with a forward tilted torso and arms hanging freely and nearly straight down and slightly out from the shoulders. The club shaft should be pointing at or slightly below your belly button. This shaft line should form a right angle with your nearly straight back [forward tilted torso] line. During the golf swing your shoulders should rotate around on the plane of your tilted forward torso [nearly straight back] for a quality swing.

Check this setup position with mirrors and make some slow swings to see the shoulders rotate around the forward tilted torso. The shaft of the club should cross over your shoulder at the completion of the backswing.

Setup without a club and with your arms crossed over your chest. Rotate the shoulders to feel the movement of the shoulders; don't let the hips move vertically. The hips and knees should support the rotating torso with near zero vertical motion. Moving vertically will cause poor club contact with ball. Practice rotating shoulders without a club, check rotation with mirrors.

The swing plane will change slightly with different length club shafts. Maintain the nearly straight back plane at a right angle to the club shaft and rotate the shoulders for a quality swing and solid contact. If you start to hit behind the ball or top shots check your swing plane.

Slow Backswing

Assume your proper setup and alignment position with an iron and no ball, soft arms extended slightly out with a short iron. Slowly rotate shoulders [only] about a correctly tilted upper torso with no hip movement or wrist hinge; club should go back on an extended target line ~ one foot. **Practice.**

Rotate Shoulders to Torso Limit to Create Torque – Assume correctly tilted upper torso setup position without a club; place your crossed arms on your chest. Slowly rotate shoulders without a hip turn, keep lower body in setup position, turn shoulders to > 60 degrees without pulling your body off balance, and feel the coiled core tightness. Rotate chest center from a 6:00 position at setup to an 8:00 [60 degrees] position; feel the coiled core. **Practice.**

Next, slowly swinging a seven iron from 6:00 position to an 8:00 position, you should feel the same coiled core tightness. **Practice.**

Wrist Hinge – Combine an upper torso rotation, coiled core, with a wrist hinge. Assume a quality tilted torso setup with a seven iron; this position has the club head at 6:00. Rotate shoulders [only] until hands are at 7:00 with no hip turn. Club head should be pointing to sky. Continue shoulder rotation until hands are at 9:00 with minimum hip turn. At this position wrist should be hinged to a near complete position [80 to 90 degrees]. Continue rotation to the three-quarter position. At this position the spine angle [tilted torso] should be the same as at setup, and the upper torso should feel like it is coiled up tightly. Practice backswing with a full-length mirror to check body/wrists at key positions. **Practice.**

Important: You should ensure that the coiled core, feel the swing engine, is tight with a straight back on a forward-tilted torso. Understand that this completed [three-quarter] backswing position is vital to all quality [effective and efficient] shots—feel the position.

Important: Head moves slightly to keep balance during swing. Head moves to the right during the backswing, and it moves slightly forward as upper body rotates

toward impact zone. This description is for right-handed golfers.

Forward Swing

Swing from backswing position to a completed forward swing position by uncoiling the body.

Take club back to 9:00 position, turn hips to left to initiate torso/body rotation and swing down through the impact position. Initiate the hip turn smoothly and then increase rotation speed.

Forward Rotation Practice – Take a stance with a short iron placed across your chest and hold it with your arms folded across your chest. Rotate to your natural full backswing position [coiled torso] and then slowly initiate a forward swing by rotating the coiled torso forward to uncoil it through the impact zone to a finished position. Repeat this practice drill until you are sure your feet are grounded to support a balanced swing, with the torso and hips rotating toward the target. You should feel your weight shift to the back leg and then to the forward leg. At the finish, the knees should be touching, with your belly button pointing toward the target. **Practice.**

Forward Rotation with an Eight Iron – With the eight iron, swing to top of backswing. Uncoil the torso by turning hips forward through the impact zone and continue rotation until knees touch, with the forward leg straight and the club head behind your head. Almost all of your weight [80 to 90%] should be on your forward foot. Your belly button should be pointing to the target or slightly left of target. Swing slowly to get the feel of the uncoiling action and swinging through the impact zone to a high finish. Increase forward speed gradually until reaching the maximum swing tempo for a balanced swing. **Practice.**

Forward Arm Close to Chest Check – Set up with an eight iron, and place a glove or small towel under forward armpit. Swing back and forward slowly between three-quarter positions the glove/towel should not drop when swinging in either direction. **Practice.**

Maximum Balance Swing Tempo – Set up with a five iron, and perform a quality back and forward three-quarter swing. Once the swing feels natural, increase the swing speed to find the maximum balanced swing tempo you can achieve. **Practice.**

Finish Position

At the "Finish Position," the back leg should touch the forward leg at the completion of a full swing, and the belly button should be pointing at the intended shot target.

Setup position – Turn back foot out ~ five degrees and the forward foot should be turned out 20 to 30 degrees. Bend from the hips and push your butt out past your shoe heels. Flex your knees and keep your back straight. Arms should be loose and hanging down; now place your arms across your chest.

Finish Position – Rotate hips back slowly from a setup position to a half-swing position. Rotate hips forward slowly from the backswing position to the finish position. The back foot should lift as you turn through the impact zone, and the back leg should touch the forward leg at the finish. The back foot should be resting on its toes with most of your weight on your forward leg. Are you in the finish position? Check with a mirror.

Repeat setup and finish positions many times

without a club until it feels like natural motion. Use a mirror to check setup and finish positions. **Practice.**

At Home Full-Swing Mechanics Check

Use short iron to practice swing fundamentals at home.

1. Setup Position – Using mirrors, take your stance; ensure a forward body tilt and that the back shoulder is lower than the forward shoulder. Ensure weight is evenly distributed between your feet.

2. Initial Backswing – Take club back to a 7:00 position with a shoulder rotation and no wrist hinge; check for smooth takeaway.

3. Slight Wrist Hinge – From setup position swing back to a 8:00 position, and verify club toe points up and there is a forward body tilt; swing club and verify a low finish position [3:00 to 4:00 position] with club toe pointing up and body tilt maintained; mirror check.

4. Wrist Hinge – Swing back from setup position to a half-swing [9:00] position; check wrist hinge with shaft pointing to sky; mirror

check.

5. Full Backswing – Swing back from setup position to three-quarter swing position; check wrist hinge with forward arm across chest, shaft pointing upward, and feel torque in core; mirror check.

6. Swing Trigger – Swing club back to 9:00 position, and initiate downswing trigger; verify smooth forward swing initiation and that arms respond to forward body rotation.

7. Touch Legs – Swing club back and forward to get feeling of both legs touching at finish.

Note: Use mirrors to check swing positions.

Driving Range

Body and Target Alignment – Prior to taking an alignment position [address] relative to the ball, a near-field ball target should be selected along the line between the intended target and the ball. This near-field ball target is used to align the clubface, shoulders, and feet to the target line. It is more accurate than trying to align oneself to a distant target.

Note: Use a stance and ball position

alignment tool to practice setup positions.

Alignment Tool Practice at the Driving Range –
Clubface should be square to initial ball flight line.

1. Lay a straight fiberglass or plastic rod on the ground, on a line pointing directly at target.
2. Lay another rod on the ground, parallel to first rod, with an eight- to ten-inch separation. This rod should be close to your feet.
3. Lay another rod on the ground, perpendicular to the two parallel rods and slightly ahead of the mid-length position of the other two rods; this rod will aid in ball and feet positioning. Ensure it will not be hit by a club or the ball.
4. After setting up to the rods on the ground, slightly behind the perpendicular rod, check body alignment, then swing several types of clubs to see and feel the swing bottom.
5. Hit several balls to validate your setup and alignment.
   - If balls fly toward intended target, your shoulders and feet are aligned properly.
   - If balls fly off intended target line, check

shoulder and feet for alignment.
- If ball continues to fly off the intended line, check swing technique [slices, hooks, pushes].

Swing Mechanic Check – Use setup and alignment tools, and take two practice swings before hitting each ball. Log results.

1. Swing Trigger – Swing club back to a 9:00 position, and initiate the downswing trigger; verify a smooth forward swing initiation and that arms are passive and respond to the forward body rotation.
2. Wrist Hinge – Swing back from the setup position to a half-swing [9:00] position; check wrist hinge with shaft pointing to sky; swing through the ball and verify a quality finish position—check for a relatively straight ball flight.
3. Full Backswing – Swing back from the setup position to a three-quarter swing position; with forward arm across the chest, feel torque in the core. Swing through the ball and verify a quality finish position—check for a relatively straight ball flight.
4. Put It All Together – Practice quarter, half,

and three-quarter swings and shots; check for quality finishes [knees touching and belly button pointing at target] and a relatively straight ball flight.

5. If ball flights are consistently flying off intended target line, perhaps a minor adjustment to your setup is necessary to compensate for a flexibility issue.

6. Log distances after sufficient practice and confidence are achieved.

Impact Position

After developing an efficient swing, some time should be spent discussing and understanding the impact position. Many instructors identify the right or left hand as controlling the clubface during impact. I believe, as do some instructors, that the hands work as one cohesive assembly and that the point of impact is approximately 300 microseconds in duration. The ball is on the clubface for such a short time that manipulation of the two is virtually impossible. However, one should look at the grip position of the leading backhand and the trailing palm at setup. The relative position of the hands as they grip the club does control the clubface during the point of impact solely as a function of holding the club, as the hands and wrists unhinge naturally through the impact position. In most cases, the position of the clubface at address will be the position of the clubface with a quality swing.

The club head should sweep across the mat or grass at the impact position. The club head should not drive into the mat or ground at impact. You want the bottom two lines on the face of the club head to make contact below the equator of the ball as the club head sweeps through the impact position. Making contact with this method will get the ball to rise without additional help.

Note: Shoulder injuries occur in players who consistently drive their clubs into the back of the ball and the ground or mat.

Achieving a balanced swing with a smooth tempo should permit an uninhibited release of the clubface through the impact point. Once your grip, setup, ball position, and swing become natural and repeatable, the ball flight should become predicable and consistent. If the ball flight is not as desirable after all the swing practice, do not change a good grip. Perhaps the ball position or swing bottom, impact point, is not exactly where it should be at impact. Adjust the ball position slightly, at the driving range, to improve the impact point and subsequently the ball flight.

There will be times when anxiety over a difficult shot influences your swing thoughts and flexibility. Remember, tension is the enemy of a quality shot. Keep the grip and arms soft throughout the swing. Do not reach for that extra yardage [firmer grip = tension] with a particular club; change the club and swing smoothly to achieve the desired yardage or ball flight.

There will be many times during your golfing experiences that the ball does not come off the clubface with maximum energy. This could be a personal flexibility or strength issue on a particular day. Swing feel is a very important influence on swing dynamics; take practice swings to achieve a swing feel for the day or shot. The ball position on the ground should influence where the swing impact point will be for a quality shot. You may have to choke up on the grip, bend the knees more, or move your setup position relative to the ball position due to ground conditions on the course.

Important: A balanced swing will produce a repeatable quality swing through the impact point.

Find Your Swing Tempo

This is an essential characteristic of a solid golf swing. Using a seven iron or eight iron, hit balls to targets 10 to 20 yards apart. Practice by varying the swing speed back and through impact to a finish position. Swing speed should be the same in the forward direction as it is in the backward direction. Transition between swing directions should be unhurried. See if you can vary swing speed while having a good swing tempo. Follow these suggestions to find your ideal swing tempo. Limit practice sessions to stay focused.

- Conduct swing tempo test with a five and/or six hybrid at 140, 150, and 160 yards. Is the ideal swing tempo the same as with the 8I?
- Conduct swing tempo test with a five and/or seven wood at 160, 170, and 180 yards. Is the ideal swing tempo the same as with the 8I?

Important: Swing tempo should be the same for all clubs.

Note: You do not have to have a perfect swing to make solid contact; you do need a balanced swing with good tempo.

Monthly Swing Check

Quarter Swing – Use an eight iron for a swing check. With a good setup, swing an iron back slowly to a one-quarter swing position. Club head should be pointing to the sky. Weight should be mostly on the back leg. Next, initiate a forward swing by slowly shifting your weight forward and rotating the hips toward the target until the back leg just touches the forward leg. Maintain the forward upper body tilt with a straight back throughout this partial swing; the club head should be pointing to the sky at both ends of this swing. The wrist should have rotated through the impact position as the hips turned to allow the club head to rotate. Use mirrors to check this wrist and arm rotation through the impact position. **Practice.**

Half Swing – Use a five iron or five hybrid to practice. With a good setup, swing the iron back slowly to a one-half swing position. Club shaft should be pointing toward the sky. Weight should be mostly on the back leg. Next, initiate a forward swing by slowly shifting your weight forward and rotating the hips toward the target until the back leg touches your forward leg. Maintain the tilted forward upper body with a straight back throughout this partial swing; the club swings naturally to a position behind the head at the completion of the swing. The wrist should have rotated through the impact position as the hips turned to allow the club head to rotate. Use mirrors to check positions, and hold the swing finish for several seconds. **Practice.**

Important: If the hands are not soft, they will not hinge properly on both sides. The firmer the grip, the more tense and restrictive the arms become. Tension is the enemy of quality shots.

Ensure the hands remain soft throughout the swing so a wrist hinge occurs naturally in the backswing and the forward swing. Keep the forward arm close to the body during the swing. Let hands freely hinge during the

backswing, unhinge freely at impact, and hinge again after impact.

Note: During the swing, I sometimes think the following to synchronize my swings. Back – "Slowly Turn Shoulders" and Forward – "Shift, Turn Hips."

Full-Swing Summary

You probably agree with me that a sound golf swing is paramount to making successful shots and the game of golf enjoyable. Keep your swing very simple for success.

You must practice to sustain a quality swing. You cannot practice swing mechanics on the course. Go to a driving range at least twice a month.

Practice to Achieve Success,
Control Emotions to Focus,
Focused Practice = Consistency
Consistency = Success
Success = Enjoyment

Game Guidance

Pre-round Strategy

Average golfers do not spend much time with Pre-round Strategy sessions. For the most part, they spend little time thinking about their upcoming round. Where is the time for such an activity? However, this lack of mental preparation often causes the strokes to add up; some of those strokes could have been avoided with some forethought on the upcoming round.

Developing a pre-round strategy is essential to playing at our maximum potential. While individual strategies will be different, some of the common elements are:

- Set objectives for the round or for the front nine and for the back nine,
- Plan a hole-by-hole strategy (avoid hazards, layup, use three-wood off specific tees, and play one fairway side or the other),
- Prepare for each tee shot (driver, fairway

metal, hybrid, or iron), and
- Lay up on specific holes to score well.

After you set your objectives, start thinking about the specific steps toward achieving them. Most courses have Web sites with course scorecards, yardage books, and hole layouts. Familiarizing yourself with hole details should help minimize errant shots. If you take the time to develop a strategy, then implement the plan to save strokes.

Pre-round Warm-up

Arrive at the course with sufficient time to stretch the muscles and warm up the swing. Performing stretching exercises for 10 to 15 minutes will save a pulled muscle, and protect shoulder, back, hip, and knee joints. The stretching exercises will also save some strokes on the first couple of holes.

Spend time at the driving range to warm up the body slowly through a progressive swing process. A suggested set of warm-up steps are listed below.

- Practice $\frac{1}{2}$ swings with pitching wedge
- Practice $\frac{1}{2}$ and $\frac{3}{4}$ swings with nine iron
- Practice $\frac{1}{2}$ and $\frac{3}{4}$ swings with seven hybrid
- Practice $\frac{3}{4}$ swings with three and five woods
- Practice $\frac{3}{4}$ swings with driver

Warm-up Critique

- Is there a setup or swing issue?
- Are swing tempo and swing balance okay?

Tension-Free Golf

Golfers do not have to stay focused on their game for the entire 4.5-hour round. They can relax and enjoy the course environment and their fellow golfers for most of the round time. For many years, golf experts have stated or implied that golfers should spend an average of 30 seconds in the execution of each golf shot. This "golf shot execution" period includes the preparation [20 seconds] and the execution [ten seconds] of the golf shot.

Using this recommended shot execution time, scratch golfers need to concentrate on their game approximately [72 shots x 30 seconds / 60] = 36 minutes per round. Bogey golfers need to concentrate approximately [94 x 30 / 60] = 47 minutes. The other nearly three hours per round should be enjoyed in a tension-free atmosphere.

Scratch golfers need to isolate all outside thoughts and focus on their current shot for ten seconds; this singular focus period consumes 12 minutes per round. The singular focused time for bogey golfers consumes about 16 minutes. Golfers should be able to concentrate for these short execution time periods; they need to train themselves to isolate their thoughts and be positive in the shot moment.

Pre-Shot Routine

Most average golfers do not have a standardized pre-shot routine. They may make the same moves every time they take a shot, but it is not a disciplined routine. There should be a standard routine a golfer steps through for each shot to help focus on only the shot at hand. A golf shot has two distinct and separate mental states, described by some golf experts as 1) out of box and 2) inside the box. Golfers should isolate all thoughts, comments, and noise while executing their shot, and focus only on target alignment, stance, and the golf swing. The execution state is characterized as "being in an isolation box." Hence, there is the shot preparation (shot assessment and target selection), which occurs outside the box, and second, the actual shot execution, which happens inside the shot box.

One should assess the ball environment [lie, slope] and the selected target location [hazards, slope, ball roll, target distance] and have full confidence in the target selection, shot type, and club selection prior to completing the first step [20 seconds] and advancing into the shot box. It is very important to separate the two elements for shot success.

The shot execution should have a singular focus, and that is the actual swing. There should be no thoughts regarding hazards, the last bad shot, small greens, or anything else. Once in the shot box you should only concentrate on two steps. First, focus on clubface alignment, ball position, and stance. After you are set up, move to step 2: focus all your thoughts on executing the best swing of the day and make the shot. The suggested pre-shot and shot steps are listed below for clarity.

Outside the Box

1. Assess the slope and ground conditions where the ball lies,
2. Stand behind the ball, select a target location,
3. Assess the course conditions at the selected target location,
4. Estimate distance to the selected target,
5. Determine best shot type to reach the intended target,
6. Select a club, perform a couple of practice swings to feel the shot,
7. Select a near-field alignment target along the flight path, and

Inside the Box

8. Filter out all distractions,
9. Step to the ball, place clubface behind the ball, and align the clubface to the near-field target,
10. Align yourself to the near-field target,
11. Take your stance relative to the ball and target line,
12. Dismiss all non-swing thoughts,

13. Look at the target one time, and finally
14. Execute the best golf shot or putt of the day.

You need to determine the best pre-shot routine that works for you. Practice the pre-shot routine until you are comfortable with it and it becomes your automated shot routine.

Note: Sometimes there is a significant amount of time waiting on the group ahead of your group. You could execute the "out of box" steps while waiting. Do not initiate the "inside the box" steps until it is clear for you to execute a shot. Sometimes it is best to start the shot preparation with the "out of box" steps to restart the golf focus after a long wait.

Swing Thoughts

Swing thoughts should be positive while thinking about target line, a relaxed, smooth takeaway with an unhurried downswing to a good finish. Some examples of swing thoughts are:

• Slow and easy

- Smooth tempo
- Finish the swing

Swing thoughts should not be focused on the swing mechanics.

Practice Putting Green

Prior to starting your round, make a few practice putts to feel the speed of the green. Most practice greens are maintained in a like manner to the course greens. Therefore, using some sage advice passed on to me, the green speed can be determined before the first tee. Use four balls to conduct the following test on a flat section of the practice green.

1. Place a tee into the ground as a reference point for your putts.
2. Set up to putt the first ball with your normal putting stance, take the putter back to a position just inside your back foot, and make a putt. Make sure your putter goes forward to your forward foot. Note the distance the ball rolls on the green.
3. Next, set up to putt the second ball; take the putter back to a position half the

distance of the first putt and make the putt. Make sure the putter goes forward the same distance that it went back. Note the distance the ball rolls on the green.

4. Repeat step 2 and 3 with the two remaining balls. Note the distance each putt rolls on the green.

5. Measure the putt distances by walking off the distances. Average each of the two [long and short] specific putt distances. This should help you determine how far to take the putter back for lag putts during the round. If time permits, repeat steps 2 and 3 one more time.

Note: The above process should save several strokes per round.

Shot Feel and Timing Adjustments

Sometimes the swing timing and feel are just not there for specific clubs. This will happen more often as we become more experienced in life. I assume you are like most golfers and you have an iron, hybrid, and a fairway metal that are your feel-good clubs. When this swing discomfort occurs, take your favorite iron, hybrid, and/or fairway metal and make some practice swings. When the timing and feel are where you want them with your favorite club, note where your hand position is relative to the distance from the club head. Change clubs to the one with the problem and place your hands on the troubled club at the same location relative to distance from the club head. This should provide a similar swing feel as your favorite club when you make some practice swings. Keep your hands at this length for the remainder of the round. You will not give up much yardage; your shot control should increase.

Another method to fix a shot control issue is to reduce the backswing and execute half shots. You may have to make half shots for several holes to regain the feel and confidence.

Reducing the backswing speed works wonders to correct an over aggressive downswing that has crept into the round.

Golf Round Record Keeping

Keep records of each round played as long as you want to improve your golf skills. If you want to improve a specific golf skill, some knowledge of your current capability is important. Analyzing the current state of the skill should indicate the improvement techniques to be addressed and practiced. Monitoring and recording specific skills in future rounds will provide the visibility regarding the expected improvement.

To better understand the state of your game, the most important statistics to record during a round are:

- Greens in regulation [GIR] on all holes
- Number of putts
- Tee Shots in fairway

To reach a single-digit handicap the following statistics should be recorded and analyzed:

- Iron shots to green
- Hybrid shots to green
- Fairway metal shots to green
- Chip shots to within three feet of hole
- Pitch shots to within three yards of hole
- Putts over 25 feet to within two feet.

Analysis of recorded data will highlight one or two

areas where improvement is necessary to reduce scores. The form below is a good model to follow for record keeping; you could make this with simple spreadsheet software.

FRONT										
Shot Record	1	2	3	4	5	6	7	8	9	Total
Driving Distance										
Fairways Hit										
Greens in Regulation										
Quality Pitch										
Chipsaves										
Sandsaves										
Putts										
BACK										
Shot Record	10	11	12	13	14	15	16	17	18	Total
Driving Distance										
Fairways Hit										
Greens in Regulation										
Quaity Pitch										
Chipsaves										
Sandsaves										
Putts										

This shot recording method could be used in addition to the scorecard. To keep it very simple, the attributes of the shot record form can be integrated into the typical scorecard. You could keep your own record while someone else records the scores for the group playing the round.

Hole	1	2	3	4	5	6	7	8	9	IN	TOT	HCP	NET
Blue	365	323	178	307	358	371	342	373	170	2787	5574		
White	351	310	144	301	343	323	330	325	162	2589	5178		
Gold	4	4	3	4	4	4	4	4	3	34			
Handicap	5	9	8	4	1	7	3	2	6				
Score	4	5	3	4	5	4	6	3	4	38			
Putts	2	3	1	2	2	2	3	1	2	18			
Notes	G	F	S	F	G	F	C	C	G				
				G									
	I	I		I	H	I	I	I					
Red	326	310	126	300	339	320	330	319	162	2532	5064		
Handicap	5	9	8	4	1	7	3	2	6				

Fairways Hit = F
Greens in Regulation = G

Chipsave = C
Sandsave = S
Quality Pitch = P

Second Shot Club
Iron = I
Hybrid = H
Fairway Metal = M

Mental and Physical States

Mental State

When you want something badly enough, you make a plan to reach the goal and execute detailed steps necessary to accomplish the goal.

Repetition of the right thing, done the right way, transforms inconsistent performance into something dependable and repeatable.

Gaining confidence in the putter, wedges, and short irons will reduce your handicap substantially through a balanced improvement.

Smooth and balance shot execution will lead to more GIRs and game enjoyment.

Making the current shot the best shot of the day is the only thing you can control on a golf course.

The game of golf illustrates your best and

sometimes worst characteristics.

Golf is a game for life; enjoy the environment, fellow golfers, and yourself.

Physical State

Sustaining one's golf skills requires routine, disciplined practice sessions. In addition, one must have a regular physical exercise program to maintain a healthy body. Golf is a contact sport requiring retraction and extension of muscles and joints in fractions of a second. Golf shots require a smooth, flexible swing to enable the club head to make repeatable contact with the ball along the intended swing path. Without a moderate amount of strength and flexibility, a golfer is susceptible to chronic pain, injury, and an inconsistent swing.

As we become more seasoned, our joints become much more important to sustaining a healthy and happy life and a golf game. Having experienced significant shoulder tears, shoulder surgery, and chronic lower backache for years, I now understand and appreciate the benefits of exercises to maintain flexibility and health.

An exercise program should include exercises to

maintain flexibility and a moderate amount of strength. Moderate strength and flexibility will protect joints and muscles in shoulders, back, elbows, wrists, knees, and hips from serious injuries.

There are many exercise programs, books, and DVDs available that address exercises for golfers. Katherine Roberts has a very good book titled Yoga for Golfers.

**Get into an exercise program
to protect yourself.**

Pace of Play

With a new or reacquired golf swing and much improved short-game skills, the golf round tempo becomes a very important element with sustaining your swing tempo. Sustaining a good swing tempo is desirable and necessary to keep you in the game and to score well.

You should become aware of any changes in your swing tempo, swing feel, or shot focus during a round. If you are playing in a slow group or behind a slow group, it will be difficult to manage your shot focus and game strategy. Playing a round of golf in five or more hours will challenge the most focused among us to stay in the game. Waiting to make the next shot each time you approach your ball will destroy your enjoyment of the game.

Here is a list of some of the contributors to a slow pace of play.

- Start time intervals less than ten minutes apart [minor impact]
- Golfers emulating the slow play of pros as seen on the TV every weekend [major contributor]
- Course length and complexity and playing from the back tees [major contributor]
- Golfers using the golf cart as a taxi [moderate impact]
- Golf course designs [moderate impact]

How does each of these contributors influence the pace of play and your enjoyment of the game?

1. Start intervals closely spaced at less than ten minutes can contribute to slow play when groups begin to cluster at par three and short par four holes. Golfers can become disgruntled with the groups in front of them, and then their intrinsic swing tempos can become erratic. Stay positive to keep your game.
2. Golfers watch the professionals on TV and think by emulating the pros' behavior, they're playing the game as it should be played—slow and methodical. A bogey golfer who takes a

long time to assess the shot conditions and options is seriously affecting the pace of play, because the bogey golfer typically shoots 36% more shots than a professional golfer.

3. Golfers typically have large egos that surface when playing with friends. Most golfers play from the wrong tees for their capabilities. Consequently, their scores rise rapidly with course length and complexities. Golfers who cannot drive their tee shots or hit their second shots long and accurately should move up to a less challenging tee area. This move will normally reduce the course complexity along with the course length, which should reduce the bogey golfer's score and play time.

4. Golf should be played as a game for walkers. However, most golfers prefer to rent a cart. Golfers use the golf cart as a taxi to travel from one ball position to another. If one of the golfers would get out of the cart, take a few clubs, and walk to his/her ball while the other golfer is executing a shot, significant round time could be saved. Besides, the walk would be good for the golfer.

5. Golf courses are becoming longer and have more environmental areas and fabricated rough areas. Courses should provide more information at each tee area regarding distances to environmental areas, hazards, and rough areas. This would provide information so golfers could choose to lay up and then hit over the course challenges. Lower scores and less playtime should be achieved by the average golfer. Golfers would also waste less time looking for lost balls.

Let Us Play Ready Golf

Ready golf is a play method to reduce the average time a group consumes during a typical round. The key element of ready golf is taking your shot as soon as you are ready, and there is no interference [group] in front of you. Here are a couple of examples to describe how it is played every day.

Tee Area – The first member of the group who has selected a club and target area steps up to the tee area and executes his/her shot when the landing area is clear. The next golfer who is ready steps to the tee area and executes his/her shot.

This continues until all golfers have completed their tee shots. Sometimes the short hitter will tee off first to save time while the group ahead advances further to clear the area for the long hitters.

Fairway – The person who is ready and clear to advance his/her ball shoots first. The next person who is ready shoots, and this process continues until all golfers are on the green. There is no priority given to someone who is further out from the hole unless two people are both ready to shoot.

> **Note: Fellow golfers are assessing the lie of the ball and shot options and selecting a landing area while one golfer is addressing and executing a shot.**

Greenside and on the Green – The player who is ready to shoot executes the shot while others are determining the slope and roll of their next shot. Ready golf is practiced until all balls have been holed.

With this method, golfers typically minimize

the time in shot assessments and pre-shot routines. Etiquette is not violated if all golfers agree to play by this method and they are respectful to each other.

Ready Golf and Golf Carts - Players practicing ready golf will get out of the cart, take a few clubs, and walk to their ball. After executing their shot, they normally walk toward their partner's ball. Most of the time their playing partner will pick them up en route to his/her ball.

Golf Scores - Most golfers playing ready golf enjoy the game more mainly due to being able to sustain a game and swing tempo throughout the round. Their scores also reflect playing with a better swing tempo.

Enjoy your game whether playing ready golf or honor's golf.

Part One
Final Word

Following the guidance in this document during my recovery has improved my swing tempo feel and timing significantly. My short-game shots are very good with increased confidence. I limit my swing to three-quarters to maximize the shot quality. I hope you have acquired a balanced swing with smooth tempo and good timing of the natural wrist unhinging at the impact point for your swings. I intend to use this reference for all my future swings and shot improvements and calibrations.

Feel the swing,
Stay balanced,
Trust your natural swing tempo,
and
Enjoy the game.

Part Two

Factors Influencing Average Golfers' Skills and Scores

If you are interested
Or curious about factors
Influencing the average golfer's
Ability to improve skills and
Score well, then these
Sections are for you

Introduction

P rimary emphasis within this part of the book is on discussing how golfer skills, practice, practice facilities, golf clubs, course architecture, course conditions and setup, and course information influence the average golfer's skills, scoring capabilities, and enjoyment. Average golfer scorekeeping and handicapping are also discussed.

Should golfers be categorized as three classes based on their basic skills or approach to the game? Golf has become attractive to many people for many different reasons; it is truly a game for all ages.

Amateur Golf and Golfers

Competitive golf provides the more skilled and driven players a venue to challenge their natural abilities against the course conditions. Professional and amateur golfer scores are compared to determine who best adjusted to the course setup and natural conditions during each specific tournament. Their enjoyment comes from rising to meet the challenges of the course and succeeding in the competition amongst their peers.

Recreational golf is played weekly or monthly by average golfers looking to socialize with neighbors, coworkers, or league members in a slightly competitive or leisurely round.

Along with discussions of potential improvements for the average golfer, there is a subtle message that the pace of play could be improved through minor changes to how courses are set up for daily play and which tee area is selected for play.

There is a generation of baby boomers advancing toward the great age of retirement. This large group, 78 million, is educated, healthy, and has more disposable income than previous generations. Is the golf industry ready to offer them a pleasant environment to learn and enjoy the game?

Throughout this section is a belief that most average golfers would prefer to shoot lower scores and improve their enjoyment without a great amount of effort or time. Most average golfers have careers and family obligations that are much higher than golf on the priority list.

Golfers are very similar in character to other sports groups. There are the professional tour groups, golf course professionals, professional instructors, amateurs, and average golfers. For as long as I have played the game, more than 36 years, there have been two categories of golfers: the professionals and the amateurs. Perhaps there are three general categories to characterize golfers: the professionals, the amateurs, and the average golfers.

For the purposes of this discussion, I will briefly describe what I perceive as the differences between an amateur golfer and an average golfer. An amateur golfer maintains a United States Golf Association [USGA] handicap index for the primary purpose of competing in competitive golf governed by local and regional golf organizations. Club golfers also maintain and work to sustain a handicap index for competitive golf within their clubs and between clubs. An average golfer, as stated before, plays the game primarily for the recreational and social benefits and the modest competition between friends and associates.

Amateur Golf – Amateur golf is organized and managed under the guidance of the USGA. The USGA serves as the national governing body for amateur golf in the USA. The USGA acts in cooperation with national, regional, and local golf associations of common interest in amateur golf. Most of the local and state amateur tournaments are organized and managed by state or regional governing groups associated with the USGA. To participate in these events, one must have an official USGA handicap index.

An official handicap is recorded and maintained by a golf course, golf club, or other organization. These organizations use a scorekeeping system software, which follows the requirements of the USGA concerning recording golf scores and computing a handicap index for each member.

There are many amateur tournaments throughout each region of this great country. Tournament information regarding qualifications, registration, and schedules can be obtained from local and regional amateur organizations; check the Internet for names and addresses within your county or state. There is a World Amateur Golf Ranking System determined by R&A Championships Limited.

I have not seen amateur golf events advertise in local papers, on regional TV, or radio broadcast. Perhaps the popularity and support for amateur golf would improve with some local or regional advertisements.

Amateur Golfer – An amateur golfer must receive no compensation or benefits directly or indirectly from his/her skills or reputation. Handicap [flights], gender, juniors, and seniors subdivide amateur golfers.

I believe an amateur golfer is more likely to be one who maintains an official handicap for participating in tournaments. Amateur golfers are usually very talented, committed to sustaining or improving their current skills, and enjoy competitive golf more than social golf. Their handicaps are usually close to zero, and they are in the top 1% of all nonprofessional golfers.

What makes up an amateur golfer may be somewhat ambiguous to most golfers. The amateur golfer needs to have acquired a high degree of skills associated with the short game in addition to putting and full-swing shots. Anyone seeking to join an amateur circuit needs to understand it is far more than playing for a club championship. An amateur's skills are demonstrated by success at competitive levels in local, regional, and national competitions. Sustaining a competitive skill level at different levels of competition gives an amateur recognition and a reputation. Gaining regional or national recognition requires endless hours of practice and numerous competitive wins per year.

Becoming an amateur golfer is not for someone who is not highly motivated and dedicated to continuous learning. Becoming very well versed in the rules and regulations of the local and regional governing organizations is essential to success, along with one's game skills.

Average Golfer

Average golfers have very productive and satisfying lives outside of golf. Average golfers can be described as avid, obsessed, dedicated, casual, talented, and a hacker. Average golfers play the game of golf anywhere and usually every week; some play once or twice per month. There are essentially two groups of average golfers: 1) avid, low scoring, and moderately talented, and 2) the recreational, casual, or leisurely, less avid golfer.

Avid Golfer

1. Low Scoring Golfer – Handicap less than nine, plays and practices regularly, plays golf > 50 times per year, and is in upper 6% of amateur golfers. The quality of their game is important to the moderately talented, semi-serious of the average golfers; these are the golfers who have time for practice as well as playing.

2. Pro-active Golfer – Handicap and skills are very important [handicap 8 to 18], reads endless books and magazines, practices and plays weekly, and is always looking for ways to improve one's game. Thirty percent of amateur golfers fit this description. Some will purchase new clubs and/or a driver each year so that they will have the latest toys of the game. Others will go for a lesson or a set of lessons each year; little practice time

usually follows due to family and work commitments.

Average golfers who shoot less than 90 per round usually maintain a handicap through some form of a scorekeeping system. These are the more avid golfers who play and practice more and are, therefore, more successful at the game.

Recreational Golfer

1. Occasional Golfer – Has very limited time for golf and almost no time for practice, scores 90 to 110, and plays golf one to two times per month. Approximately 40% of amateurs are in this group.
2. Retired Golfer – Handicap [10 to 36] is not important, reportedly looks at golf as Getting Old and Living Fine. Plays golf one to two times per week. Nearly 24% of amateur golfers are partly or fully retired.

A handicap is an indicator of how well one is supposed to play. This is probably true for the amateur and semi-serious average golfer. However, causal golfers, most retirees, and most recreational golfers do not want to participate in a handicap tracking system. These recreational golfers move the ball to a better position [out of divots, off bald spots, etc.] prior to executing a fairway shot. They also move it out of bunker footprints. It should be stated that most public courses are resource-limited in keeping divots repaired and bunkers raked.

Many groups play the game in a relaxed and casual manner. Their scores are only a measure of how well each golfer was able to manage the challenges of the course and to provide talking points for the 19th hole. How does one measure one's capabilities or calculate an accurate score or handicap average? Perhaps the majority of leisure golfers are on the course for enjoyment rather than as competitors. Their scoring average is unknown and in most cases unimportant. This casual, average golfer makes up the majority of weekly patrons at public and daily fee courses.

Are you an avid or casual golfer? You need the same skill types to play; the more practice, the higher the probability of lower scores. Each type of player can equally enjoy the game.

Playing the Game

This game measures success, enjoyment, and satisfaction by one's score. Most activities in life are measured by some acceptable standard, and for most participants the score is a good measure of one's experience. The score provides a means to compare one's performance against the course to another golfer's performance. With professional golf transmitted to nearly every home for their viewing pleasure, most people believe a par score is the true measure of success.

A highly skilled golfer is expected to score par on each hole. The highly skilled player should be able to two-putt from almost anywhere on the green to complete a hole. The highly skilled player should be able to reach any four-par green in regulation with a tee shot and one approach shot. A five-par green should be reached with three shots and with two putts; a score of par is achieved. When reaching greens in regulation, the skilled golfer should score par for each hole.

For the average golfer, a bogey should be the standard that the majority of golfers should compare themselves to with respect to playing a challenging course. There is a simple USGA formula to determine the bogey rating of any course; however, the bogey rating is almost never posted. With the majority of golfers averaging greater than 92 for a round, it seems like a score of bogey would be an acceptable measure of satisfaction for any hole and any round.

The majority of the average golfers play from tees that make the course too challenging for their intrinsic skills. Average golfers should consider using tee areas where their average tee shot puts them within reach of the green in regulation. If you want to improve your scores, answer these questions and change the tee area used for your rounds.

1. What club do you use to reach the green more than 60% of the time from the fairway when you make a full shot?
2. What distance does your average drive carry when you hit the fairway?
3. Add the average distances from questions 1 and 2.

This is the average length of par-four holes for

you to regularly score a bogey. Why did I say bogey? Average golfers miss most greens due to accuracy issues. You will probably make a par 50% of the time using the distance from step 3. If you play longer length par-four holes, your probability of making a bogey increases.

Everyone Wants a Good Score

SECTION TWO

Golfer Skills

Confidence in one's game comes from balancing golf skill improvements in these essential elements: mental, physical, driving accuracy, full shot consistency, short-game skills, and putting.

Most shots executed by golfers are within 100 yards of the green. In an 18-hole round, approximately 70% of an average golfer's shots (66 of 94) are in the scoring zone, < 100 yards to the green. The 70% includes putts, bunker shots, chip, and pitch shots. Table 2.1 illustrates the average shot types per game per handicap type golfer. These data were collected from golfers playing thousands of golf rounds. Does your game closely match what is illustrated in Table 2.1? It seems that acquiring a feel and skill for short-iron shots should be a priority to improving one's handicap. Another way to look at the information is to believe that improving one's accuracy at hitting fairways and greens would reduce the number of short-game shots needed per round.

Table No. 2.1: Shot Type Averages per Golf Round

Golfer	Score	Putts	Full Shots	Short Game
Tour	71	28	26	17
Scratch	72	30	27	15
10 Hdcp	83	34	25	24
20 Hdcp	94	36	28	30
30 Hdcp	105	39	29	37

The average golfer's ability to hit greens in regulation can be biased by the inappropriate use of tee areas. This could make the approach shots too long for one's skills. Studies of low-scoring, average golfers have implied that if golfers improved their ability to hit greens in regulation [GIR], their scores would improve. Other studies have illustrated that as a golfer improves their GIR, their putts per round increase.

Golf instructors have stated correctly and with some bias that improvement to GIRs, short-game skills, and putting will lower scores. I would submit that improving the ability to place full-swing shots [tee, fairway, and approach] at or very near the intended target area is equally important. I believe that a golfer who wants to shoot below 90 must have a balanced set of skills to meet the multiple challenges architects incorporate into the course designs. Table 2.1 indicates that most golfers who attain a lower handicap have balanced the improvements by lowering shots in each area. Having an unbalanced set of skills where one sprays the tee shots and/or misses most greens in regulation will surely stress the other game skills to score. This type of erratic play will lead to sustaining high scores and frustration.

If average golfers would play to their strengths, use the best tee area for their intrinsic skills, strive to keep it in the fairways, and work on the short-game shots, scores would fall rather quickly. Most average golfers can play a round with fewer than 38 putts. I would suggest putting improvements could be deferred until the other skills have the average golfer scoring in the mid 80s.

The USGA and others have conducted tests and recorded the average tee shot and iron shots of large groups of golfers to arrive at average shot lengths for different skilled golfers. With these data, golfers' abilities have been categorized relative to shot distance and a typical four-par length hole. I have taken the liberty of making a table out of the information for ease of illustration. If one desires to score well and enjoy the game more, the data in Table 2.2 should be helpful in identifying the best tee area for one's intrinsic skills.

Table No. 2.2: Average Shot Lengths
and Course Yardage Table

Player Type	Tee Type	Handicap	Average Score	Average Drive	4-Par Hole Reached in 2 Shots	Course Yardage Rating
PGA	Black	0	< 72	275	525	> 6900
Amateur	Blue	< +4	< 76	250	470	< or = 6900
Average Low Handicap	White	< / = 9	< 82	225	420	< or = 6600
Average / Bogey	Green	< / = 18	< 91	200	370	< or = 6300
Bogey +	Silver	< / = 24	<98	175	325	< or = 6000
Double Bogey	Gold	< / = 36	<110	150	280	< or = 5700
Double Bogey +	Red	> 36	> 109	125	240	< 5400

- The "Average Drive" column and the "4-Par Hole Reached in 2 Shots" column contain information implying the shot length consistency to score pars on typical par-four holes of this yardage.
- The "Course Yardage Rating" column, right

most, suggests the average course length one should play to score well with the full shot capabilities of the two columns to the left.

- The first, third, and fourth columns identify and describe the scoring abilities of different golfer categories.
- The second column suggests the tee type to be used with specific capabilities described in columns four, five, and six.

Summary

The golf course architecture and daily setup can significantly contribute to an average golfer's ability to score well. If average golfers would play to their strengths, use the best tee area for their average drive and approach shot lengths, and strive to keep it in the fairways, the course challenges would become more manageable. Improving one's short-game shots will reduce scores rather quickly.

Play to Your Skills

SECTION THREE

Practice and Practice Facilities

Finding a high-quality practice facility is vital to the process of rejuvenating one's game skills.

Most average golfers have limited time for practice due to more important priorities of family and career. In most cases, the only available practice facility is the local driving range. Without a quality short-game practice venue, it is difficult to learn and refine a balanced set of short-game skills. This is the primary reason the average golfer's handicap has not changed in the past 40 years, while the game has increased in popularity. Just imagine if the highly talented doctors, scientists, engineers, teachers, firemen, policemen, and others were to spend half as much of their overtime at a quality short-game practice facility as they do at their professions. Golf would have millions of golfers with handicaps below ten.

Focused Practice

Average golfers do not spend very much time practicing the short game. When they do have a small amount of time for practice, they head to the accessible driving range to hit middle irons, fairway woods, and the big dog. Close to zero time is spent on putting or chip and pitch shots.

The reason most average golfers spend little time on their short games is primarily due to the lack of facilities with short-game practice areas. Most driving ranges have hitting areas with a durable mat as the practice ground. Practicing multiple types of shots from the same type of ground interface—mat—does little to excite the eye and hand sensors.

Golfers should investigate the availability of short-game practice facilities with public access. If you find an accessible short-game practice area, consider yourself very fortunate.

Golfers should not spend their limited practice time attempting to refine only one skill element of their game. Balancing practice time with the near-green [chip and pitch] shots, bunker [greenside and fairway] shots, and fairway shots will keep the session interesting.

One should have a single focus, such as swing tempo or swing balance or setup and alignment, during a practice session. It could become frustrating and nonproductive to attempt multiple changes or to focus on multiple swing thoughts during a practice session. Improvements come in small steps but usually last a long time once learned.

No one element [driving, approach shots, short game, putting] of anyone's game will significantly reduce a handicap permanently. Skill improvements in multiple elements of the game bring lasting results to one's handicap. Each improvement will reduce scores a few shots because it is exercised only a fraction of the time during a round. If an average golfer were to spend 50% of their limited practice time on one or two skills, such as acquiring a short-game skill or an improved approach shot accuracy or driving accuracy, it would pay significant dividends. One to two hours of focused practice per month could easily change a double-bogey golfer into a bogey golfer or a bogey golfer into a single-digit handicapper.

Few of us are natural golfers who require little practice time to play well. The professionals and the top amateurs could play well without much practice for some time. However, they would not be satisfied with just playing well. Practice is essential for everyone while developing new skills in any endeavor.

Quality practice and practice time are essential to improving and sustaining basic golf skills. Any golfer's practice session should have a clear and singular purpose with an obtainable objective. Practice should be viewed as an opportunity to learn new skills rather than as boring. Practicing golf techniques is an experience in creativity; when new skills are learned, confidence increases along with satisfaction.

Practice Facilities

How much could the average golfer improve with ready access to a quality, multifaceted, short-game practice facility?

A quality and accessible short-game practice

facility with multiple areas designed to improve one's short game, bunker play, and shot accuracy would be a great benefit to average golfers. Access to a short-game practice facility could significantly improve one's ability at stroke-saving skills and short-game confidence. This type of venue would change a significant number of bogey golfers into single-digit handicappers.

A practice facility with a chipping green and another area with several greenside bunkers to practice chip and sand shots would be very popular with all golfers. Add a short-iron practice area with yardage markers at ten-yard intervals for golfers to practice pitch, lob, and other short shots, and the facility would have to schedule practice times to meet the demand of all golfers. Being able to observe the length, flight, direction, and repeatability of short-iron shots would increase one's confidence in making quality shots to the greens during each round.

There are very few driving ranges or golf courses with a short-game practice area or a practice bunker set aside for public access. A rare facility has a practice green or area available to refine chip and pitch shots to improve placing shots near the flag. A facility that had an area with multiple yardage markers out to 50 yards would be marvelous. This type of area would help golfers to practice short-pitch and lob shots. It would be wonderful if a practice facility had markers every ten yards out to 100 yards to practice short approach shots and to make mental notes of the fly distances and shot accuracy.

Summary

A regional practice facility with quality short-game areas would probably do more business than local driving ranges. An area with a couple of bunkers to practice shots to a green would really be in demand by average golfers. Another practice area with a chipping area and a pitching area to a green would be in demand for practice time. Access to such a facility could lower average golfer scores after a couple of visits.

Quality Practice Makes Quality Shots

Golf Swings and Clubs

Confidence in your capabilities when using irons or fairway woods is critical to enjoying the game. How can average golfers increase confidence and control of their shots?

O ne of the skills that separates the amateurs and the professionals from the average golfers is the ability to make solid contact with the ball during full swings. Average golfers typically have more difficulty with longer clubs, and because of limited time to practice, the balanced swings become more erratic as we mature.

Golf Swings

Average golfers have swings that for the most part vary with different clubs. Some swings become more erratic with longer clubs, and some golfers feel they must swing harder with a longer club. This harder swing is an attempt to increase shot distance because the club seems to be ineffective at slower speeds.

It has been my experience, and that of my fellow golfers, that one or two clubs in the bag are easy to control. These become the go-to clubs to get out of thick rough, and back to the fairway. Since average golfers are limited in available time for golf, these go-to clubs must naturally match their individual physical composition. The shaft length matches the arm length and body type and the ability of the average golfer to make a full swing. Usually the go-to clubs are the 5-6 or 6-7 or the 7-8, depending on the golfer's height, flexibility, and body type. If the average golfer has one to two irons, a hybrid, and one fairway metal that suits their game, why not the other clubs? It must be the shaft length difference that makes them more difficult to control and swing; let us assume the clubs are from a matched set. Again, the average golfer does not have sufficient free time to work on acquiring a better balanced swing skill.

I believe the erratic swings increase in frequency due to a lack of strength and flexibility as one becomes a more seasoned player. The arm swings of our youth are more difficult to control with decreased strength. To sustain the intrinsic skills as one passes beyond 40, a change to a core rotation swing becomes necessary. This can be a difficult transition; most average golfers accept the increase in their scores as normal. As golfers age, they need to protect their arms, shoulders, and backs through exercise to prevent muscle and tendon stress tears. Most average golfers accept the golf swings that are intrinsic to their physical composition.

Golf Clubs

What would happen if golfers were to hold the other clubs at the same distance from the club head as their favorite clubs? I tried this with my fairway metals after I realized that "The Club" had shorter shafts. It is my belief that the shorter shafts provided increased control, which was the selling point of The Club. I gained more shot control by choking down one to two inches to make the fairway metal shafts shorter.

The transition golf sets that recently appeared in golf stores have lighter weight shafts to facilitate placing more mass in the club head to increase lift and control. Transition club shaft lengths start to increase in length over traditional iron sets above the eight iron. The three through six in most transition sets appear to be similar to hybrids in shaft length and club head designs. Transition sets are very good for the average recreational golfer and the more mature golfer.

Hybrid clubs are designed to improve one's ability to get the ball on a better flight and thus gain more shot distance. They are designed to have shaft lengths close to being in the middle between fairway metals and irons with the same loft angle of an iron. Average golfers like them because of the improvement in shot control and distance over irons. For some average golfers the hybrids are difficult to control; perhaps it is the increase in shaft length over the equivalent iron club.

I believe the average golfer would benefit from a set of clubs with shorter golf shafts. As an example, if the four- and five-iron shafts were the length of the six-iron, shot control would increase. Perhaps most average golfers would gladly trade the control for a slight loss in distance. I should point out that if a golfer is topping, slicing, or hooking one's shots, having more control should increase distance with solid shots.

Fairway metals as well as hybrids could each be made with one length shaft per club type for better shot control. One length seven-wood for fairway metals and one length five-hybrid for hybrid clubs would increase shot control for the average golfer.

Most manufacturers sell shot length [power golf] over control to feed the golfer's ego. I would think manufacturers could fabricate sets with two distinct shaft lengths for most average golfers. The manufacturers have mechanical engineers to calculate the distances and probable control factors. It would probably take one or two simple alterations to their current club performance algorithms and model software code to determine the best shaft length.

However, using a modern mechanical swing test machine that can be adjusted to match the nominal swing characteristics of an average golfer will probably indicate the benefit to average golfers of single-length shafts. The average golfer, who likely does not have a balanced swing with ideal swing tempo, will probably benefit immediately if the shaft length and flexibility match their favorite club.

Golfers may want to see if reducing the shaft length on their irons to the same length as their favorite iron improves shot control. Golfers can do this by determining where they hold their favorite club that produces the best shots and mark the location of the top hand on the shaft. They could place a piece of tape at the same location relative to the club head on the other clubs. They could then go to the driving range to see the improvements in shot control and perhaps distance as well.

I would suggest that they initially use a different length for fairway metals and for the hybrids from the irons and then check the performance of the altered [taped] shaft length clubs at a driving range.

If they are pleased with the performance of the irons and not with the hybrid and the fairway metal performance, a minor adjustment to the hybrid and fairway metal length may provide satisfaction. They could increase the hybrid shaft length one-half inch or one inch more than the favorite iron to see if they gain control and solid contact. After becoming comfortable and pleased with the results, they could lengthen the hybrid and fairway metal shaft distances (move the tape) in steps to find their specific shaft control length.

Summary

It seems like increasing shot control and perhaps even distance through more solid contact would be a great benefit to the average golfer. Golfers would quickly learn the new shot distances for the revised clubs and celebrate increased control and the lower scores.

It seems like there would be a large market for a set of shot control clubs for the more mature golfers. In addition, these golfers could best afford the purchase of a new set of clubs. Let the standard long-shafted clubs go to the young, flexible, and strong power golfers.

Have Confidence with All Your Clubs

A Golfer's Eye for Course Details

Course architecture challenges the mind as well as pleases the eye. Do you appreciate and understand the subtle changes in hole and green undulations or slopes?

Golf Course Architecture

Most people believe that a well-designed golf course should have holes that allow golfers to use every club in their bag during every round. Golf courses should be like puzzles (challenging holes) where one has to put different-shaped pieces (shaped shots) tightly together to finish (score well) the puzzle. Course architecture should challenge the mind as well as please the eye. A significant number of recreational golfers enjoy the natural beauty of golf courses and the animals that live within their surroundings.

Does the average golfer look for the design centerline of each hole? Most times golfers are not aware that the architect has laid out each hole with a predetermined method to score par and one or two more challenging paths to be rewarded with birdie if the risks are avoided. Centerlines are used as reference lines of varying lengths to lay out fairways, position hazards, initiate dogleg turns, and position greens. Elevation changes between the tee area and the green usually follow the natural terrain changes of the land prior to the development of the course. In most cases, if the average golfer is able to follow the course centerlines, a very good score will probably be realized.

Par-three holes will have a straight centerline from the back tee area to the center of the green. Sometimes the tee areas are designed to point in a slightly different direction to challenge one's attention to detail and to add a degree of difficulty to an easy hole. An elevation change and sloping terrain with some water feature also will influence one's vision of the hole and its perceived difficulty. Hazards and undulating greens are used as a final measure to protect the short hole from countless birdies and pars. Mother Nature, over time, has protected par-three holes with large trees and overhanging branches at the tee areas and near the greens. As average golfers mature and lose strength and flexibility, a yardage of 175 yards or less is a sufficient challenge on most days.

Par-four holes usually have a two-section centerline path. In the past, there usually was a shift in the direction of the centerline at approximately 250 yards. This was followed by a straight centerline to the center of the green. Most modern course designs have eliminated the dogleg in favor of power golf. I believe this has reduced the need to be aware of the environment on most modern courses, and reduced the mind game significantly.

Modern courses have slight alterations in the direction of the centerline, which should not be classified as a dogleg. Holes should have centerline direction changes of greater than 30 degrees to be classified as doglegs. Most long hitters can totally ignore the slight change in direction on modern courses. The first centerline segment of a par-four hole typically represents the average tee shot length or 200 to 250 yards. The length of the second centerline segment typically represents an approach shot length of 75 to 200 yards to the green center.

The architect incorporates hazards, slopes, narrow fairways, water, environmental areas, and thick rough to increase the risk and reward attributes of most par-four holes. Incorporating tee box misalignments, forced layups and carries, sloped and undulating fairways, as well as rolling greens adds to a hole's character.

Par-five holes usually have a three-section centerline path. Par-five holes are designed in a similar manner to par-four holes. The difference is the second segment is usually the length of the typical approach shot segment of a par-four hole. The third centerline segment of a par five is usually 50 to 125 yards. Architects use methods similar to par-four holes to add difficulty and challenges to a typical par-five hole. Some par-five holes may have two doglegs; this is a rare feature.

Natural contours, fairway slopes, and green undulations enhance the natural beauty of a golf course. Most architects will preserve much of

Mother Nature's design while designing hole layouts and producing a golf course. Alterations to the natural contours are necessary to maximize drainage, enhance visualization, and to challenge the golfer's mind and shot skills.

Modern golf courses are designed to be environmentally responsible and to protect the habitat for wildlife and plants. There are natural limitations and regional restrictions concerning water management, drainage, environmentally sensitive areas, and habitats. Most courses are integrated with the natural environment while presenting desirable playing conditions. Course maintenance is vital to balancing natural beauty with playability and golfer enjoyment. Golfers should recognize and appreciate that golf courses are managed land areas that enhance the natural beauty of an area.

With the natural beauty presented by golf courses comes play restrictions that must be respected and adhered to by golfers. Signs are usually posted at the tee area to identify and define any sensitive areas, accessibility limitations, and play restrictions. Signs are intended to aid the golfer in planning how to play the hole. Good signs will define the distance to a layup area and the distance to carry over the sensitive area. With these signs, golfers will better enjoy the hole and its surroundings.

The next time you play a round. Take some time while waiting for your turn to examine and enjoy the course environment.

Enjoy the Course Layout and Surroundings

Course Conditions

Courses present a fair test for the majority of the patrons and a balanced challenge to the short-game skills of all golfers. Do your game skills match the challenges of your home course?

A re golf courses set up for a fair and modest skills test for the average patrons, bogey golfers, or are courses set up for the low handicappers?

Seventy-three percent of public and daily fee course patrons score greater than 90. Less than seven percent of the public and daily fee patrons score below 80. Are golf course setups too difficult for the average recreational golfer to score well?

Should golf courses be set up to provide a fair test of skills for the majority of customers and a reasonable pace of play? Here are some examples of conditions that can add significant difficulty, strokes, and play time to the average golfer's round.

High Rough Adjacent to the Fairways – It seems that public courses are eliminating the intermediate height cuts on most fairways. Average golfers miss greater than 60% of fairways. Eliminating an intermediate cut will add minutes to the playtime, searching for balls a few yards off the fairway on nearly every hole for an average foursome of golfers. Most times, you cannot see the ball until you are directly on top of it. Consequently, the high grass can add three to five minutes per four- and five-par hole to find two to four balls. This could easily add 24 to 42 minutes per round.

High Rough Adjacent to the Greens – Public courses are cutting the grass surrounding greens to heights of four to five inches. This high grass is a means to sustain the difficulty rating for the hole. Average golfers miss 50% of greens with their approach shots. Extra thick rough results in very difficult shots, sometimes two shots, to egress the rough. Players having difficulty finding and extracting a ball out of this thick grass can increase scores and playtime by 13 to 26 minutes.

Unmaintained Areas – Areas separating adjacent holes and underbrush at the edge of the woods, cleared of debris for a considerable distance, improve the course beauty and playability. Average golfers spend a significant amount of time, 15 to 30 minutes, during a round in these areas looking for their errant shots. Without any white stakes, these areas are in play, so one has to find an escape path to the fairway. In a significant number of shots, the archer [golfer] has difficulty controlling the arrow's [golf ball] flight off debris, under tree limbs, or around the trees and bushes. Thus, shot counts increase for the average golfer as well as playtime.

Bunkers Need Daily Maintenance – Escaping from someone else's footprints, yesterday's shot tracks, or from overly packed damp soil adds unnecessary difficulty to bunker shots. Average golfers would like to have bunker conditions that are a fair test of their abilities. Bunkers should be raked daily to minimize yesterday's evidence and to loosen the soil after storms. Maintaining the bunkers daily enhances the playability of the course and adds to the enjoyment of the round. If bunkers look unmaintained, customers probably will not practice self-maintenance when exiting the bunker.

Fairway Divots – Patrons of public golf course are mixed about replacing large divots, filling in the divot holes, or doing nothing. Full divot mix/sand bottles in the carts at the beginning of a round improve the likelihood that patrons will assist in repairing shot scars. Empty mix/sand bottles in carts at the beginning of a round sends the message that the staff is not serious about repairing the scars of play.

Mix/sand bottles should be located at one of the tee areas on each par-four hole [10 of 18 holes] so golfers see them and replace the empty bottles while waiting or preparing for a tee shot. Placing replacement mix/sand bottles in fairways of holes where the soil is exceptionally susceptible to scarring is a good reminder to golfers.

Ball Marks – Some patrons are either forgetful or reluctant to repair ball marks on greens. The average golfer misses 50% of the greens with their approach shots. Repair of ball marks from chip shots is usually unnecessary; this probably is why a significant amount of ball marks are not repaired by golfers who occasionally hit the green. Golfers need reminding to perform self-maintenance on the course; par-three holes are a good location for a sign: "Repair Your Ball Marks." A good sign at the starter shack is "Show me your divot repair tool to play."

Forced Layups and Carry Areas – Modern golf courses are designed to be environmentally responsible and to protect the habitat for wildlife and plants. Courses must be integrated with the natural environment while presenting desirable playing conditions. Course maintenance is vital to balancing natural beauty with playability and golfer enjoyment. Golfers should recognize and appreciate that golf courses are managed land areas with natural limitations and regional restrictions concerning environmentally sensitive areas. Upscale, daily fee courses post signs at the tee area to clearly define any sensitive areas, accessibility limitations, and play restrictions.

Summary

Average golfers who practice to gain accuracy and consistency with their drives, full-swing shots, and approach shots can avoid most trouble areas and hazards. One should play conservatively to avoid problems and score well.

Are conditions for forced layups and carryovers conducive to the average [shorter] hitters? A forward tee and a low-risk landing area may be necessary to accommodate the weekly recreational golf groups. The additional tee area and a bailout landing area should reduce scores, speed up playtime, reduce lost balls, and increase player enjoyment. There are many areas where changes to the course, some inexpensive, could enhance the pleasure of the average, short-hitting golfers and improve the pace of play.

The more difficult a golf course plays for average recreational golfers, the more golfers improve their ball positions. The recreational golfers are not at the course to compete; they are there to enjoy the atmosphere and their fellow golfers. However, increasing one's score also increases one's playtime even if the additional strokes are forgotten when recording a score.

A properly maintained course looks appealing and adds to the pleasure and enjoyment of a golf round. A well-groomed course is highly desirable to customers in a competitive market. When average golfers are fairly tested and score reasonably well at a course, it will be placed on the repeat play list.

Fill Divots,
Rake Traps,
Repair Ball Marks,
and
Play to Your Strengths

SECTION SEVEN

Handicapping Average Golfers

Average golfers could use a simple standardized scorekeeping system for their recreational golf.

G olfers who play several times per week and have handicaps below 12 tend to have a USGA handicap index. Most average golfers [>90%] at public or daily fee courses do not maintain an official or unofficial handicap average and do not know with some degree of accuracy their average score for the current season. Golfers who play infrequently, one to two times per month, have high handicaps and usually have an erratic scoring pattern that can vary up to eight strokes per round.

Why are there not two official handicap systems? One system, the USGA handicap system, for professionals and serious amateurs, and another system for the average/recreational golfer.

After-work golf leagues and a significant number of weekly leagues use their own scorekeeping systems because they are simple to implement, understand, and provide a reasonable reaction to erratic play. These scorekeeping (spreadsheet) systems vary from recording and averaging the gross scores to subtracting par from the gross scores and averaging the differences. Most of these systems average the last three to ten scores with no distinction between low or high scores. Most of the recreational golfer scorekeeping systems do not account for course slope in determining handicap differentials. Some of these systems segment the golfers into flights by scoring abilities.

For leagues where average scores are greater than 92, having a scorekeeping system that averages the last four to six rounds provides a reasonable average to match against fellow golfers with nearly the same game skills and scores. Scorekeeping systems that average more than six scores will tend to smooth out the erratic rounds and may not be a true reflection of the high-scoring recreational golfer's current game.

Recreational golfers and league players want to play golf, socialize, and have fun. They want to start competing as soon as possible after the league play is initiated for the season. They do not want to wait until the sixth round to get a handicap. League players need a scorekeeping system and handicap at week one to have a friendly competition. They want to be able to discuss their rounds and flight position at the water cooler.

Most league players want to understand how the handicaps are calculated. Understanding the handicap calculation and seeing periodic reports usually satisfy most league players that the scorekeeping method is fair. Large leagues will organize golfers into flights based on skill levels. This way golfers within a flight play against each other rather than with someone who has a significantly different handicap. Giving a fellow golfer a large number of strokes [> 5] in a nine-hole match can work on the lower handicapper's head.

Most group and league members play golf once per week. Group and league scores are maintained within scorekeeping programs that are less rigorous than the USGA handicap system. Most leagues use the last four to six scores to determine a weekly average for each member. Using only the most recent four to six scores in the database to compute an average handicap helps the more erratic of the league players by having the handicap average reflect the highs and lows of one's game over the past month. Using a system that averages the ten lowest of the last 20 scores does not support the erratic play of recreational golfers. Most recreational golfers do not play 20 rounds per year.

Some will argue that the simple spreadsheet scorekeeping methods lack accuracy in determining a true handicap. Recreational golfers roll the ball out of divots, off bare spots, out of footprints in bunkers, drop a ball at a point adjacent to where the previous shot became lost, and take other liberties. Some of these actions are justified by the maintenance condition of some public courses. Accuracy in handicap calculations is relative to the group's playing rules; recreational golfers want to enjoy the environment and their fellow golfers.

It is difficult to find a semi-automated scorekeeping software product for leagues where players participate once per week. Most scorekeeping and handicap calculating software products are advertized to be equivalent to the USGA defined method. There are a few products for group and league scorekeeping. Most of the product descriptions are vague, so it is difficult to assess whether the product will suit one's needs for recreational golfers or if it is another version of the USGA method.

Another view looks at the serious golfer and professional golfer playing four rounds per week or 20 rounds in five weeks. The league golfer plays once per week or five times in five weeks. So averaging a recreational golfer's last five rounds is relative to a professional's last 20 rounds—nice stretch.

Average Golfer Handicap Estimator Method

Here is a fairly simple and accurate handicap system for recreational golfers that I use, which can be easily implemented on a PC.

1. Record member's gross score.

2. Check to ensure each gross score is within +/- 40% of current handicap average plus par rating of course and tee played. **See note 3.**
3. Record gross score if within 40% limits defined in step two, or record the gross score limit defined in step two as the adjusted gross score.
4. Compute handicap differential using the adjusted gross score.
5. Compute handicap average, average last **n** handicap differential records, where **n** is the number of rounds the league members selected to be averaged. This can be any number from four to eight. **See notes 4 and 7.**
6. The computed handicap differential is the handicap average for the next round. **See notes 5 and 6.**

Notes:
1. This simple and accurate handicap system can be incorporated into any spreadsheet software as an Average Golfer Scorekeeping Record.
2. There are two filters to limit erratic scores from affecting one's handicap average. Each

has its merits and each can be set to any value to minimize weekly variances in handicap averages. It really depends on how social or competitive a league wants their golf game.

3. This scoring filter limits any unusual gross scores. The limit should be set to match the statistical variances anticipated by the average member of the league flight. Filters for different flights could be: A = 30%, B = 40%, C = 50%, D = 60%, and other flights could use 70%.

4. The lower the value [n] the more the handicap differential reflects erratic scores. The higher the value [n] the less reactive the handicap differential is to a really good or bad day.

5. Setting the gross score filter at a low percentage [<40%] and/or setting the number of handicap differentials [n] above six will make the scorekeeping system less for social golf and more for competitive golfers.

6. This system does not account for the difficulty or slope rating of each course. Adding slope to the handicap differential

calculation is very simple.

7. Selecting the number of rounds to average for recreational golfers should match the number of rounds the average league members play per month.

Note: Golfers should use the tee area that best matches their golf skills.

Scorekeeping Examples

Don Duffer

1. Don has a handicap average of 11. His most recent league score was a 49 on a course where par is 35.
2. Don's gross score limits for the course are +/- 40%.
   a. [35 + [11 x 1.4]] = 50
   b. [35 + [11 x 0.6]] = 42
3. Don's adjusted gross score equals his gross score of 49.
4. Don's handicap differential is 49 – 35 = 14
5. This league averages the last four differentials. Therefore, the most recent three differentials are 13, 9, and 12. Add the most recent differentials and determine the average. [13 + 9 + 12 + 14] / 4 = 12

6. The handicap average for the next round is 12.

Steve Slice

1. Steve has a handicap average of 8. His most recent league score was a 47 on a course where par is 36.
2. Steve's gross score limits for the course are +/- 30%.
   a. [36 + [8 x 1.3]] = 46
   b. [36 + [8 x 0.7]] = 42
3. Steve's adjusted gross score is set at the upper limit of 46.
4. Steve's handicap differential is 46 – 36 = 10
5. This league averages the last four differentials. Therefore, the most recent three differentials are 8, 10, and 7. Add the most recent differentials and determine the average. [8 + 10 + 7 + 10] / 4 = 9
6. The handicap average for the next round is 9.

Summary

Average golfers who play in groups weekly would like to have a simple method to record and track their scores. They are satisfied with using all the actual scores or differentials rather than the lowest of half the scores. Most simply would enjoy having some record to discuss and compare with fellow golfers. If most of the golfers within the group are playing with the relaxed rules, the score records have relevancy without absolute accuracy.

Enjoy Each Round

SECTION EIGHT

Golf Course Information

A course's essential information can enhance one's enjoyment and score at an unfamiliar course. Take advantage of yardage books and course signs to play holes smartly.

Quality signage contributes to a golfer's pleasurable experience at an unfamiliar course. Effective communication is essential to enhancing one's enjoyment and improving the perceived playability of an unfamiliar course.

High-quality, concise tee signs recommend the best tee area relative to one's intrinsic capabilities at full shots. These signs usually identify distances to specific fairway direction changes, hazards, water, and drainage areas.

Most upscale courses provide yardage books to convey detailed course information to patrons; these books provide information for each hole relative to layup and carry distances, environmental sensitive areas, or natural hazards. Yardage to bunkers, hole directional changes, and green centers are detailed for tee shots and fairway shots.

The game's pace of play improves with quality tee signs and yardage books; knowing what is over the hill or around the corner improves one's shot choices. When golfers understand the hole characteristics at an unfamiliar course, they generally play better golf and spend less time looking for balls from errant tee shots.

A golfer's enjoyment increases proportionally with the communication style of a golf course. Knowledge improves one's attitude toward any given course. Golfers generally ignore small, wordy signs.

Moderate daily fee courses have similar yardage books for sale, usually less than $10.00. Most municipal courses have limited yardage signs, and few have yardage books.

Course directional signs should be clear, with

indicators to the next hole, restrooms, bag drops, restaurants, parking, and other necessary information to facilitate an enjoyable day.

Take Advantage of all Information, Score, and Enjoy the Round

SECTION NINE

Colored Stakes on Golf Courses

How many golfers understand the use and meaning of the colored stakes and lines used throughout a golf course?

S takes communicate course conditions; an understanding of the signs would facilitate proper use of a provisional ball and a more effective pace of play.

White Stakes and White Lines – Used to indicate **"Out of Bounds."** The inside point of the stake at the ground is the boundary line. If a painted line is used, any part of the line is out of bounds.

- A golfer must assess a **one-stoke penalty** if a shot goes out of bounds. A golfer must return to the spot of the previous shot and hit the next shot.
- To save valuable time, a golfer should always hit a provisional ball if the first ball is believed to have gone out of bounds.

Whites Stakes used Inside Course Grounds – Sometimes white stakes are used on fairways and other areas to indicate **"ground under repair."**

Yellow Stakes and Yellow Lines – Used to indicate **"Water Hazard."** The inside point of the stake at the ground is the boundary line. If a painted line is used, any part of the line is in the water hazard. A water hazard typically runs across the line of play.

- A **one-stroke penalty** must be assessed if the ball is unplayable.
- There are two options for putting a new ball into play. One is to return to the spot of the previous shot and hit the next shot.
- The second option, most commonly used, is to drop a ball and execute a shot. This dropped ball must be dropped behind a point where the ball crossed the hazard line. The ball can be dropped anywhere behind the point crossed and a line to the flag on the green.

Red Stakes and Red Lines – Used to indicate **"Lateral Water Hazard."** The inside point of the stake at the ground is the boundary line. If a painted line is used, any part of the line is in the lateral water hazard. Lateral water hazards run alongside or adjacent to the line of play.

- A **one-stroke penalty** must be assessed if the ball is unplayable.
- There are two options for putting a new ball into play. The most commonly used is to drop a ball at a point where the ball crossed the hazard line, no closer to the hole. The ball can be dropped anywhere within two club lengths and then the next shot can be made.
- The second option is to cross the hazard to the other side and take a drop equidistant from the hole where the ball crossed the hazard line and hit the next shot.

Green Stakes – Used to identify **"environmentally sensitive"** areas. Check course rules on how to play balls out of these areas.

Blue Stakes – Used to define ground under repair. Usually golfers are permitted to take a free drop outside the blue stakes with no penalty. Drop must be no closer to the hole.

Red Stake and Yellow Stake [Double Stakes] –

Used to define the dividing line between two types of water hazards.

Blue Stakes with Green Tops – Identifies environmentally sensitive area being treated as ground under repair with mandatory relief. Check course guidelines.

Red Stakes with Green Tops – Identifies environmentally sensitive area being treated as a lateral water hazard with mandatory relief. Check course guidelines.

Are you prepared for the stake test?

One's Lifetime Has No Deductions
For Time Spent Enjoying Golf

Printed in the United States
215233BV00003B/16/P